UNCOMPAHGRE

UNCOMPAHGRE

by

Muriel Marshall

The CAXTON PRINTERS, Ltd.
Caldwell, Idaho
1981

Library of Congress Cataloging in Publication Data

Marshall, Muriel.
  Uncompahgre.

  1. Uncompahgre Plateau, Colo. — History.
2. Uncompahgre Plateau, Colo. — Description and
travel — Guide-books. 3. Automobiles — Road guides —
Colorado — Uncompahgre Plateau. I. Title.
F782.U5M37   978.8'39   80-11666
ISBN 0-87004-282-3

LIBRARY OF CONGRESS
CATALOG CARD NO.: 79-57240

  Marshall
    Uncompahgre.

  Idaho : Caxton Printers, Ltd.
  225 p.
  8009   791204

Printed and bound in the United States of America by
The CAXTON PRINTERS, Ltd.
Caldwell, Idaho 83605
135989

To Hal, Linda, and Crystal

CONTENTS

ILLUSTRATIONS

UNCOMPAHGRE

Chapter I

PARADOX ON ALL SIDES

ON THE WESTERN SLOPE of the Colorado Rockies the spectacular San Juan and West Elk mountains stand up in peaks, all but screaming and waving to get the attention of travelers, but the horizon-long crest of the Uncompahgre Plateau just lies there, blandly concealing its weird geology and turbulent history.

Hardly anybody outside the Slope knows about the Uncompahgre, and it has a name to match — hardly anybody outside the Slope can pronounce it. You say "Un-come-pah-gray," with the accent on the "pah," and take your pick of several translations of the Ute Indian word; "rocks made red by water," "rocks that make red water," or just plain "dirty water."

Though the place where this natural stream pollution occurs was originally one small mineral spring, the name was given to a whole tribe of Utes (against their will), a mountain, a river, and one town — which later repudiated it because hardly anybody (even *on* the slope) could spell it, opting instead for Delta.

Actually the Uncompahgre is more than a mountain, it is a mountain range — a great sky-long roller-wave crest, its strata bending up from under the Colorado River near Grand Junction, towering into the cliffs of the Colorado National Monument, running up in a long slant for ninety crow-flight miles southeastward, butting against the San Juan Range where it spurts up in snowy peaks like a surf wave straddling a rock.

You can drive an ordinary passenger car the full length of this crest.

On few mountain ranges does the easiest road run along the very top from end to end. This is only one of the paradoxes and mysteries of this strange mountain so little known to the touring multitudes that its sandy Divide Road offers the automobilist the same feeling of exploration usually experienced only by jeepsters.

The Uncompahgre Plateau rims out almost two miles above sea level and one mile above the wide valleys that parallel it on either side. Big as it is, the plateau is only the stump of a much longer, higher, older range. What geologists call the Uncompahgre Uplift extended heaven-high from somewhere around Vernal, Utah, down to Farmington, New Mexico, several hundred miles to the southeast.

As you see by your map (having a Forest Service map will pay off when we pin down some of the shenanigans of geography and cowpunchers later on) the Divide Road heads in the same general direction as U.S. Highways 50 and 550 along the Uncompahgre and Gunnison rivers, but higher, cooler, and more scenically. As both mountain and valley gently slope upward, the plateau maintains its mile lead of altitude above the highway, taking you through forests and high-country flowery meadows rather than desert and bringing you out on some breathtaking sweeps of infinity down both sides of the divide at once.

Though this skyline road is car-traversable and has little traffic, don't expect to save time by taking it — this is a road *through*, not *to*. It not only has a slower road surface but is longer and twistier and keeps offering irresistible reasons to stop and enjoy. On the paved highway you can get from Grand Junction to the San Juans in about two hours. Most people take the Divide Road in at least two one-day stages. Non-natives who are towing or toting their roofs can camp overnight or a couple of weeks at any of several campgrounds. Travelers who depend on buying lodging can take the 25 Mesa Road off the crest midway of its length down to Delta and spend the night in a motel.

There are several routes to the top of the plateau, but we will start from the north end and head southward because the colors of leaves (whether summer green or autumn gold) are more brilliant and shadows are more dramatic when you travel toward the sun. With the light at your back scenery ahead looks flat and washed out, like front-lit snapshots of people squinting into the sun.

Before we set wheels to the plateau let's take an overall look. Once up there we will have long views, vast views, and intimate vistas framed in forest, rail fences, and flowers but no panorama of the entire plateau. You can see the plateau whole at eye level from the west rim of Grand Mesa — or from below (a horizon-long wall) from almost anywhere between Grand Junction and Montrose.

The Uncompahgre is so long it looks low. Outlander pilots of light planes are dismayed to discover, sometimes too late, that frequently above the easy-looking ascent of the horizon rim, and running full length of it, is a matching roller wave of wind, created as the prevailing westerlies hit the steep wall of the west face, swoop up, crest, and curl downward on the other side, producing a continuous downdraft that can press a small plane onto the ground.

The Uncompahgre is so straight along the top it looks smooth, but that blue chalk line across the sky is no indication of the rough terrain on either side. Steep declivities, especially along the west side, are a jumble of crazy drainages.

On the east things are more organized but scarcely smoother. The mountain slants eastward from the crest like the back side of a surf wave, streaked with a riptide of canyons all running one way as if a giant comb had been raked down the slope, deep and crooked. Alternating mesas and canyons ribbon down from the rim all the way, creating a twenty-mile-deep fringe.

Starting wide at the top, these mesas pinch down to miles-long strips so narrow in places you can toss a rock from side to side. The separating canyons begin deceptively in dimples of woods or meadows at the edge of the Divide Road, growing in a couple of miles to gashes hundreds of feet deep. Roads and trails snake down many of the mesa tops, at least part way, but you can travel crosswise of the "fringe" (lengthwise of the mountain) only by horse or pack trail, except for the Divide Road along the top.

Paradoxes surround the Uncompahgre Plateau on six sides.

Above is the invisible air barrier, below is an apparent paucity of minerals worth digging for, though the mountain height is bordered with treasure — gold, silver, copper, lead, zinc, vanadium, uranium, coal, and gas and oil shale.

Along the east and west sides are the paradoxes of rivers that refuse to follow the line of least resistance by taking the easiest route downhill.

The Dolores River to the west is so flagrantly unreasonable that its point of defection is literally named Paradox Valley. Here the river, grinding along the bottom of a deep, crooked canyon of red sandstone, enters a broad easy valley and flows straight across and out the other side into the lockup of another tortuous canyon.

On the east the Gunnison River in Black Canyon gouges deeper and deeper in a slot full-length of an upthrust of black granite — like a crack in a loaf of French bread on a table — when it would seem much likelier to flow down past Montrose and along the lower and softer adobe earth of the Uncompahgre River Valley that parallels the canyon only three or four miles away. Both rivers went wrong in their youth and are now stuck in the ruts they made for themselves when peer pressures in the form of highlands long gone were very different from what they are now.

To the south the paradox is that the surface contours of the Uncompahgre seem to sweep up unbroken to blend into the slopes of the San Juan Range. But hidden between is a great curving fault that slid alien strata together, cutting the plateau off from all that mineral treasure — the gold and silver that bought the Hope Diamond, among other turn-of-the-century flamboyancies.

Bounding the Uncompahgre Plateau on the north is another paradox — Unaweep Canyon, said to be the only canyon in the world where a stream flows both ways. The name is a Ute word meaning "dividing of waters." Unaweep

Granite quarry jutting sheer above Unaweep Canyon.

Canyon is, in fact, a split across the plateau. The part that broke off tilts to the north rather than to the east, creating north-flowing arroyos in Glade Park and the beautiful red-rock formations of the Colorado National Monument. From U.S. Highway 50 and I-70 at Grand Junction you can plainly see the thick bands of strata curving up from where they got stuck under the Colorado River (or whatever real estate was piled there at the time) while the bulk of the plateau was heaving heavenward.

Unaweep Canyon contains its own miniature watershed. If you are being rained on at a certain spot deep in the canyon, theoretically half the drainage from your sombrero would find its way via West Creek into the Dolores River and half via East Creek into the Gunnison.

Now that we have cased the plateau from all aspects let's touch down and begin the trip.

Leaving U.S. Highway 50 at the little settlement of Whitewater on the Gunnison River, we head west on Colorado State Highway 141. About twelve miles into Unaweep Canyon the Divide Road, (Forest Road 402) leaves the pavement, branches to the left, and immediately tackles the canyon wall.

After switchbacks have put you on the first rim of the canyon (a gray granite ledge) watch for a rock quarry on the right. It is worth walking down the short slope to the abandoned works. Squared-off slabs, the perpendicular cavities where they were cut, drill holes, and remnants of rusty iron make beautiful abstract sculpture, framing views up the weirdly direct canyon that splits this mountain. Straight down, far below the tips of your boots, are hay meadows, ranch buildings, and cars like ants chasing each other along the highway you just left.

From this quarry, blocks of pale, fine-grained granite were cut in the 1930s and shipped to Denver to build the city hall. Stone of a slightly different color and texture went west to build a couple of San Francisco banks.

As you walk back to your car and step in a single stride from the granite to the red dirt roadbed, your legs are

Soft wild grasses and hard granite cliffs frame a view of hayfields down in Unaweep Canyon.

straddling 350 million years of time. That granite, the basement rock of this mountain, was formed upwards of 600 million years ago; the dark red Chinle mudstone that rests directly on it settled out of inland seas "only" 250 million
years ago.

Rock strata formations are the books by which geologists
read earth's history, and a lot of this book is missing. It's as
if you skipped from the first to the last chapter of *Gone with
the Wind* and threw the middle away.

Gone with the wind (and water) is the right term for
what has happened. When we get up on top and look out
across the rest of Colorado and huge sections of Utah, we
will be looking at formations put together from some of
these missing pages of history, pages that were ripped,
washed, and blown away during the hundreds of millions of
years when this mountain was doing its yo-yo thing — by
turns sinking to become sea bottom and collect layers of
rocks, and rising to become skyline and slough them off.

For several miles before and after the quarry the road
skates along on this time warp, using the granite ledge for
support and the soft Chinle for surfacing.

From Precambrian granite to the plateau's cap rock of
Dakota sandstone, your car has about a half mile of straight
up to negotiate in just a few miles of anything but straight
forward.

Wait a minute. Wasn't that Dakota sandstone back there
when you entered Unaweep Canyon after crossing the
Gunnison River? Right. Told you this is a weird mountain.
The tilt of the mountain is so much steeper than the cut of
the canyon that by the time you arrive at the foot of the
granite quarry you have about three thousand feet to climb
just to get back to where you were, geologically speaking.
The steep part of the climb will be up through the twisting,
wooded slot of Jacks Canyon, which you enter as the road
swings left away from Unaweep Canyon.

Since part of the fun of exploring the Divide Road will
be to discover how places on the map got their names (logical, whimsical, and just plain mad), it is frustrating right at

Tree pushes environment apart in getting to the top. At the mouth of Jacks Canyon.

the start to be unable to pin down the derivation of Jacks Canyon.

Some old-timers say it was named for Chief Captain Jack, a Ute subchief under Ouray, who with Chief Douglas cosponsored a wildcat protest demonstration in 1879 known as the Meeker Massacre, which was about as much against Ouray (who had signed treaties giving away tha San Juan goldfields) as it was against the white agency officials who were destroying Indian livelihood and status sources by putting game and pony-grazing grounds to the plow.

On the other hand, grammarians who note the absence of an apostrophe in Jacks Canyon incline to credit jacks of the four-legged variety, escaped and living wild in this lovely place, freed by hard times from slavery in area mines.

A short way into Jacks Canyon a road to the left branches to another quarry. This one yields the flagstone that makes many Grand Junction homes and yards so attractive. Flat stone in reds, tans, browns, gray purples and blue greens is available in countless places on the plateau. Permission to lift and haul it must be obtained from the Forest Service or the Bureau of Land Management.

About two miles after Jacks Canyon cracks the whip with a final set of switchbacks, you are out on top at an elevation of eight thousand feet, having almost doubled your height above sea level since crossing the Gunnison River bridge. But "top" at this point is so wide and flat it is as hard to get the sensation of "divide" as it is to really observe the roundness of the earth from a rowboat on the ocean. Just wait.

The "sea" here is the gray green of sagey grass, islanded with dark clumps of mixed conifers — still a straggle of low-altitude junipers and pinyon pine among high-country spruce, aspen, and "real timber" — the stately ponderosa pine. The "reefs" of mountain shrubbery are scrub oak, cliff rose, wild rose, serviceberry, chokecherry, and dozens of others which you will discover.

That little 170-foot bump to the right is Mount Unaweep, one of this peakless mountain's peaks.

To the left a reassuring Forest Service sign and an easy-looking road beckon to the Dominguez Recreation Area. At its start this road looks as car-safe as the one you are on, and for several miles it is (usually), but don't trust it far unless you have four-wheel-drive or pickup-truck power under you.

This warning goes for any side road traced in dotted (unimproved road) lines on your Forest Service map. Beginning as innocent as a June morning, they may run for miles through flowery sage and grass flats, between parklike groves of pine, fir, spruce, and aspen; but whether you notice it or not, you are gently easing down a fingering mesa that keeps narrowing as the canyons on both sides deepen and widen. Inevitably the mesa will peter out, and you'll have to turn around (if you haven't trapped your car in a tight spot where you can't) or drive down a cliff-shelf dugway that is liable to be booby-trapped with places too narrow to meet another vehicle, usually on a blind corner, places where the curve is too tight to make it without backing a couple of times, or some little spot (perhaps so tantalizingly short you can almost spit across it) that you can inch your car carefully down but too steep, stony, soggy, or sandy to drive back up with the power and road clearance of an ordinary passenger car.

You could be down there a long time before some Samaritan with more motor macho finds you and hauls you out of your troubles.

These side roads are mainly work roads used by cattlemen, loggers, wood and rock haulers, Forest Service personnel, prospectors, deer and arrowhead hunters, rockhounds, and paleontologists, all of whom drive jeeps, pickups, and other craft with compound gears.

Jeeps-only roads are not marked as such, except on the maps. This is no dude mountain with nature trails, guard rails, and danger warnings — as you noticed on the precipice of the granite quarry. Your safety, and that of your pets and children, is at your own discretion.

The mountaintop park at the Dominguez Recreation Area turnoff, like others on the plateau, is flowery from spring to fall with a succession of bloom that begins with

Moss writes hieroglyphs on Dakota sandstone — small pleasures at your feet to match the vast ones of the view from here.

sego lilies and princess plume and continues through primroses, cactus, sulphur flower, buckwheat, columbine, wild rose, phlox, daisies, lupin — too many summer kinds to name — and climaxes with blue asters and golden rabbit brush. In drought years, miniatures of all these peep from protective pockets of sand in the natural paving of lichen-mottled sandstone.

This wide glade is a good spot — one of scores along the Divide Road — to let the kids and dog out for a romp (nothing within miles to fall off of) while you sip coffee from the thermos, contemplate the sandy-rock ruts of the Dominguez road diminishing to the edge of the world in casual curves an artist might despair of inventing, and indulge that familiar daydream of someday having the kind of time and transportation it takes to turn off and unravel the secrets of every alluring side trail you come to.

The scope of country the road points to — the drainages of Big and Little Dominguez canyons — would take a lot of unraveling. As a matter of fact, nobody has ever seen it all. It is rugged terrain, especially in its lower reaches where canyons cut through the narrowing mesas to island pieces of skyline that have been named for their shape or inaccessibility as Triangle Mesa, Star Mesa, and No Man's Mesa. At the very bottom (where else?), squeezed against the Gunnison River, is Poverty Flat.

This islanding of mesa-ends, in conjunction with apparently recent courses of river rollrock, leads one amateur geologist to speculate that the Gunnison may at one time have cut back into this mountain, perhaps at a point well into Escalante Canyon, down through Cactus Park, and out the east end of Unaweep Canyon.

Do the names of places like No Man's Mesa, Poverty Flat, and Cactus Park (cactus and park? What a contradiction in terms!) stir your itchy-foot daydreams to the point of pain? Well, there is much, much more of mystery down there, never reached except by moccasin, boot, and hoof.

In the land of the two Dominguez creeks are scores of Indian camps, the earth black with centuries of campfires (one such site is eighty acres in extent) and sparkling with flint chips where arrows and other tools were made generation after generation.

Petroglyph Indian writing is frequent on cliff faces and on free-standing rocks of significant size, shape, or situation; some so weathered as to be considered extremely ancient.

There are no cliff dwellings. Dakota sandstone and other formations on the Uncompahgre do not produce the deep caves found in Mesa Verde country, but many rock overhangs blackened with prehistoric smoke indicate that the tribes took advantage of whatever shelter was available.

Down there, as in all parts of the plateau where the ground is not hidden by forest growth, flint and agate artifacts of all kinds, once ubiquitous, are still found, especially in hard-to-get-to areas — arrowheads for killing deer and people, tiny bird points, long knives, and spearheads; slender stone awls for punching holes in buckskin to sew sections of garments and tepees together with strands of sinew or whang; sharp-edged scrapers for cleaning flesh and fat from hides; metate and mano sets for grinding seeds into meal.

Stone lasts a long time, but when you see wooden artifacts you are looking at recent work. A few wickiup poles are still in place down there, and an occasional travois pole has been found, identifiable by the unique way one end wore down while being dragged behind the laden pony.

In the lower, arid part of Dominguez country semiprecious stones have been discovered — agate, opalized dinosaur bone, crystals, and amethysts, the latter associated with outcroppings of copper ore.

The plateau has the honor of providing scenery for the final violent episode in the battle for grass between cowmen and sheepmen in this whole region of the West. Near Camp Ridge down in that wilderness of branching canyons is the site of what is known as the Delta County Sheep War.

Sheep came to Uncompahgre country about twenty years after cattle. By that time grazing rights on public lands surrounding privately homesteaded springs had been informally apportioned among the cattlemen and firmly established. There were no laws, but an unwritten code drew a "sheep-line" around the mountain. Sheep — regarded by cattlemen with all the delight of finding weevils in the flour bin — were supposed to stay the hell the other side of the line.

The sheep-line from Delta to Grand Junction was the Gunnison River. In 1916 a Montrose sheepman, Howard Lathrop, hung a one-sheep-wide swinging bridge across the river between Little Dominguez and Escalante canyons and set a band of several thousand woollies to gobbling cattle grass.

Carl Gilbert, who as a teenager took part in the "war" along with his father and brother, describes it in his old age, "Now that I am the only survivor and the story can be told.

"Hundreds of cattle wintering down there would starve if the sheep ate the grass. Snow was too deep on the plateau to move the cows anywhere. Lathrop hadn't broken any laws, but he sure fractured the code of the West. Even if we did take him to court the cattle would all be dead by the time we got a decision, so we handled it ourselves."

Six of the cattlemen, after a meeting at the Musser ranch on the Escalante, rode through the night carrying rifles. Their names — which will pop up on your map and in pioneer anecdotes as you progress along the mountain — were Bill Gilbert and sons Carl and Zoe, Don Musser, John Hilkey, and Ben Lowe, a Kentucky racehorse trainer and wild-horse breaker, who at forty-seven was the oldest of the bunch by several years.

Hunkered behind rocks on Camp Ridge above the sheep camp they waited for dawn so they could see to shoot. They then proceeded to reduce the herd by a couple of hundred sheep, carefully avoiding anything human that might be in the tent.

Purely confident that they were in the right, they didn't even bother to remove the evidence, the empty rifle shells — though at least one gun (Carl's) was one-of-a-kind in the area. They trailed directly home in broad daylight, right up the middle of the Escalante Road.

The maneuver got publicity in local newspapers but no

action from Lathrop, so they tried again, ten men strong. Their numbers were increased by the addition of Bert Shreeves, Oscar Huffington, Tom Brent, and Harry Stockham, son of Delta's bank president.

This time a sheepherder showed his head, running out of the tent to saddle and ride for help. Carl and Don prevented him by shooting his mount and the packhorse.

Lathrop got the message the second time around and pulled out sheep, herder, and bridge.

Though nobody was ever prosecuted or even accused, Gilbert eased his teenage sons off to cowpunching jobs in Utah and Arizona, and he wore a gun for a while.

Newspapers incensed the cattlemen by calling them "Night Raiders," but what lingered in Carl's craw was the aspersion cast on his marksmanship when papers wrote, "They even tried to shoot the sheepherder," a charge it was impossible to refute without naming names.

"Hell, if we'd been aiming at the herder, his horse would still be alive today!"

Apparently the "war" was not quite over. It is said to have been the provocation for a unwitnessed shoot-out between a deputy sheriff and a member of the raiders — the Cash Sampson and Ben Lowe duel in Escalante Canyon the following summer. Though neither survived to explain what their quarrel was about, old-timers believe Sampson was close to proving who the riders were.

However that may be, no sheep have grazed on this side of the sheep-line to this day.

Chapter II

CARSON HOLE

AFTER THE HAIRPIN gyrations of the Divide Road in getting up out of Unaweep and Jacks canyons, Rocky Pitch is a mere squiggle in the road, hardly worth naming. But named it is. When snows, hunters, or itchy-backed cows have not knocked it down, a Forest Service sign announces this relatively unimposing ledge of rock running crosswise of the Uncompahgre Plateau.

Considering its straightness, geology buffs may speculate whether the Pitch is another crack-off of the plateau, paralleling the Unaweep but shut, not open.

The present good condition of the road down the Pitch is no indication of the barrier it presented to early-day wagoneers, who subtitled it Hellcat, among other things. If the rocks seem thoroughly cowed now, it may be as much because of prolonged blasting by cusswords as by road scrapers that in old (mule-power) days piled dirt on the sharks-teeth rocks only to have it skinned off by the next flash flood.

The first wheeled craft to make tracks the entire length of the plateau crest was the chuck wagon that accompanied the annual roundup. This two-rut crease in the grass connected "salt roads" that looped around canyons and occasionally across the top like a twisty rope thrown over a packsaddle.

The salt haulers serviced the "stomps" and "licks" of the various cattle companies — a few, such as Jeff Lick on up the road, are still identified by name. Unaided by roadbuilding equipment of any kind, the salt haulers broke the bronc terrain, dragging wagons over impossibilities, sometimes with the help of a fifth-wheel saddle horse at the end of a taut up-slope rope to keep the wagon from tipping over.

Roundup began invariably on July 9 and lasted 30 days.

The date was firm, according to J. D. Dillard who rode the roundup many times, because in pretelephone days it was easier to meet a deadline than to get word out about changes. As weather allowed, each stage of the roundup also had a specified date.

"That was so riders, say from the Club outfit or with errands in town, could know exactly when the roundup would reach their territory and be on hand to work their cows.

This rigid arrangement served another purpose in later years, enabling old cowhands to return from wherever in the U.S. and world they had migrated to enjoy a nostalgic rerun of their hard-riding youth, with no doubts about when the party would begin or just where it would be on any given date.

Ironically, the great cattle-macho roundup began at a place called Sheep Creek!

Moving up to the southend crest of the plateau near Darling Lake, the roundup worked from there northward — perhaps because, being higher, that section would get wintered in first, or perhaps because that's the way cattle first came into the country.

In the summer of 1881 stockmen in the Gunnison area, a couple of hundred miles to the east, had their herds pointed west, ready to move toward Uncompahgre virgin grass the minute the Utes were evicted in September. Some were in before the Utes were out — the Roberts Brothers east of the divide and, on the west, R. W. Johnson of the still-existing Johnson & Johnson surgical supply firm. Johnson "soonered" because he was already on the spot, having placer mining interests on the San Miguel River. Gold wasn't panning out too well, literally, so to satisfy the stockholders, or divert their attention, he shifted goals. Buying thousands of head, mostly Texas stuff, he organized the San Miguel Cattle Company that later became the immense Club outfit.

Within weeks of the eviction, dozens of other large and

small cattle companies rushed in, pre-empting the springs and streams, each taking informal "use rights" possession of as much surrounding public land as his cow population could graze in comfortable distance between drinks.

The first roundup was held in 1882, about as soon as there was a calf crop to lay lasso on.

On the big day, cowpunchers from all the southend out-fits gathered at the flats around Darling Lake, each bringing a string of three or four horses to make up a cavy of about three hundred remounts, in charge of one man.

While the chuck wagon (carrying bedrolls as well as grub) and the cavy followed the crest, riders were down on either side hazing cattle up out of canyons, forest, and brush toward designated "bunch grounds" (some of these are named on your Forest Service map) where they were sorted according to the ownership statements burned into their hides. Calves were branded to match mamas.

Each owner, or his foreman, was roundup boss while the operation worked his territory. As it moved on, he and his riders dropped out, to be replaced by punchers from cow camps down the line. Anyone who wished (or was paid to) followed the roundup the whole way. It became something of a social event — dirty, noisy, stinking, laborious, but jolly.

"There would be about a hundred men, women, and kids and a thousand dogs," J. D. Dillard remembers. "People would come out from town just to be a part of it."

Roundup humor was rough and ready.

"I remember one time when I was just a punk kid," Dillard goes on, "and Joe Landers was ropin' for the Calhoun outfit. Slocum's horse broke in two with him, there at the bunch ground. Slocum was about to fall off. The old pony bucked him over a pile of rocks, and Slocum managed to stay up. He rode him across that and fell off in the dirt on the other side.

"Joe Landers was closest to him, and everybody thought he would catch the horse, but Joe just let him go, saddle and all.

"Somebody said, 'Whyn't you catch his horse, Joe?'

"And he said, 'Hell, when a man knows he don't dare fall

off on a pile of rocks and then falls off afterwards there's no need of fallin' off atall. I thought he'd just as well be afoot!' "

Morgan Hendrickson, Uncompahgre-raised, brings up Joe's unfinal end:

"Joe and his sidekick Fred Sharp were a couple of spooks (drifters) Alex Calhoun hired to clean up the herds of wild Texas cattle he got (for free and unwanted) when he bought the Club outfit."

All cattle were untame at that time, but the "square" ones knew that when they saw a rider approach in a certain determined manner they were supposed (after a permissible show of token protest) to groove into the nearest cow trail. The wild ones, resistant to becoming beef, simply tossed their heads, snorted, and hightailed deeper into brush and canyons. Aside from the fact that they ate just as much valuable grass as *bona fide* cows, they were a corrupting influence, brainwashing tractable steers into joining their radical ranks.

"You'd lose fifteen or twenty head a year to the wild herds," Hendrickson says.

"Calhoun paid the two spooks a small wage, plus so much for each rebel they brought to the corral.

"Sometime after they got the job done Joe disappeared. It was thought he drowned in the San Miguel while pushing cattle across the swollen river. Or maybe he just faded farther west, running from something like a lot of people did."

The last big roundup on the plateau was held in 1937, by which time drift fencing (the pole-worm fences and all the cattle guards on the Divide Road) and the Taylor Grazing Act had restricted the grass-greed of cows and cattlemen, and no general roundup was needed to return wandering northend cows to their southend pastures.

A briefer, neater, but less exciting version of the "summer gathering" roundup social event was the annual Permittee-Forest Service Personnel Picnic held, until recently, at the Mudhole Picnic Campground — formerly the

Mudhole Bunch Ground. This was the more or less official end of the roundup in time and territory.

Permittees are cattlemen who have grazing rights within National Forest and Bureau of Land Management boundaries. They don't get permits for free — it costs about a third of a dollar to board an animal up here for one month.

How many head a stockman can run on public lands depends on how many his granddaddy brought in — a perpetuation of the "use rights" thing. If the original herd was a thousand head he may graze something like that figure now; if it was twenty-five he can't have any more.

Competition for grass reached self-destruct excesses when the range was wide open. Each cowman stocked his area with as many cows as he could lay cash or mortgage to and grazed to the roots. If he didn't, somebody else would. The herds were enormous. One old-timer remembers seeing fifty thousand head in one bunch held for shipment on what is now Grand Junction suburbia — The Redlands.

Overgrazing brought on regulation to save the mountain from dying, as mountains up around Gunnison died in that area. To bring grazing within the capacity of the range to maintain itself, the Forest Service gradually (and proportionately) reduced the herd population of the allotments. Grazing rights are not sold directly but are transferred to the new owner whenever a ranch changes hands.

The Mudholes area — besides having the world's most unappetizing name for a place to eat — has unhappy memories for many cowboys, one of them Morgan Hendrickson. Cattle, not noted for brains, had a tendency to graze too far in, mire fast in the mud, and die there unless rescued. Periodically somebody was delegated to ride up and "pull the bog," a term implying that it felt like a whole lot more than a critter was on the heavy end of the dally rope.

"The Government" was once pulled out of one of those mudholes. Weston Massey, son of a pioneer family whose cow camps are named on your map, tells about it:

"The first forest ranger on the plateau — that was about 1907 — had a name (it was Elmer Reed), but all the cowboys called him The Government and put him through quite a lot of hazing, him and his mule. That mule was too lazy to help the sun move his shadow, wouldn't run no matter how hard The Government tried to heel-thump him past a walk.

"But one time some cowboys sicked some dogs on him, and that really moved the mule for once. He ran right into a mudhole and almost turned a somersalt. Didn't really hurt The Government but sure slung a lot of mud on him."

You won't find the Mudhole Picnic Campground on the map. According to the U.S. Forest Service it doesn't exist, but cattle people emphatically say otherwise.

It finally became clear there was a Mudhole picnic ground, all right, but the Forest Service, apparently unable to stomach the name, renamed it Divide Forks Picnic Campground. That's down the road a piece.

The north end of the Uncompahgre Plateau is notable for its magnificent specimens of ponderosa pine, standing alone in parklike glades, scattered along rock-paved stream beds, towering over aspen clumps. The Forest Service has marked an especially grand one for you with a sign giving height 101 feet, circumference 45 feet, age 350 years.

These old giants are said to be survivors of vengence fires set by departing Utes who, when treatied out of their ancestral hunting and living grounds on this beautiful and bounteous mountain, burned the forests to leave as little as possible for usurpers. Opinions differ. Old-timers who knew Chief Ouray, his wife Chipeta, and their people, protest that Indians loved the forest too much to destory it merely to strike back at whites. But Dillard remembers:

"Indians had burned it slick. You could see cattle and deer as far away as you eyesight could make them out."

At Carson Hole Narrows, a couple of miles south of Rocky Pitch, you get your first gut feeling of driving along the fin of a divide. In places this fin is little more than road wide, the cliffs breaking sheer into canyons on either side — La Fair on the east and Gill Creek on the west. Here you are standing on another of the plateau's paradoxes: The streams in these canyons flow parallel to the crest at this point

Carson Hole — or as deep into it as you can see without walking the mile to the bottom. (Silhouette of Grand Mesa in the distance.)

(about the only ones that do), but they flow in opposite directions. La Fair flows north to empty into Big Dominguez — this junction *is* Carson Hole — and then east to the Gunnison; Gill Creek, in its wide, grassy-floored canyon, heads south before swinging toward Casto Reservoir and eventually the Dolores River via West Creek in Unaweep Canyon.

Standing at the scenic overlook on the east edge of the Narrows you are staring down into Carson Hole.

Beaver-trapper, scout, Indian-fighter Kit Carson is popularly supposed to have had a cabin down there sometime before the Civil War, a supposition reinforced by the name of nearby Beaver Creek.

In fact, the Hole is named for Old Man Carson (first name George, not Kit), a hermit type who came in after the Indians left, but just barely. He trapped, grew berries and garden sass along the creek by his cabin, bothered nobody, and asked the same in return.

If he was one of the pioneer West's prevalent loners (runaway men holed up in hideouts from something they'd done in the East) he was not too paranoic to be hospitable to those who went to the considerable trouble it took to get down there. Children, now elderly, remember being invited to help themselves from his berry patch.

His raspberries, whether naturally wild or gone wild, still grow along the creek bottom, and you can gather them if bears, birds, and squirrels haven't beat you to it.

To get to his place you drive back to the Carson Hole picnic ground (about half a mile) and walk down a steep mile-long trail to the stream. Year by year there is less and less sign of Old Man Carson's existence, but even if you don't discover any trace of his cabin the site is worth visiting for the eerie, foreboding sensation of the Hole and its canyon-depth ambience.

As you stand on the narrowest part of the Narrows, that little hump across Gill Creek, due west and about a hundred feet higher than your eye-level, is called Hungry — not Hungry Hill or Hungry Mesa, just Hungry. It says a lot about how things were when places on the plateau were

Depths of La Fair Canyon. The fatal shooting between two settlers occurred a few paces to the right of the picture.

being named. Beyond it is Hungry Gulch, a tributary of the Gill.

The roadbed of Carson Hole Narrows is enigmatic — soft, ochre-yellow sand, piled on top of a fin of otherwise naked rock. It's so soft and deep in places you could get stuck if it weren't for the passage of the road grader now and then.

Why doesn't it wash away or blow off?

Actually, it probably blows in. This may be one of the places where that roller wave of wind along the crest, losing carrying power in the dead air of the back-curl, dumps its load. In view of how many times a year the Western Colorado sky turns a dense yellow or red — the color depending on which Utah real estate is airborne — it is remarkable there are not more blow-sand deposits and duning on the downwind side of the Uncompahgre crest.

On La Fair Hill, just beyond Carson Hole Narrows, one of the plateau's most poignant tragedies occurred. Ted Lockhart tells about it:

"I was punching cows for one of the northend cattlemen in those days. A feud between two men of different cattle outfits had been building for a long time. Not part of any cattle-sheep war, or anything like that. Over nothing in particular, just personalities.

"Well, those two men met on that hill, and one of them pulled his gun on the other. The man looking into the barrel of the gun had his son along with him, a little kid not six years old. He pulled the kid up in front of him and said, 'Don't shoot the boy.'

"But after a while his arms got tired, and he had to let the boy sag a little. Shot got him full in the face, right over the child's head.

"Killing didn't stop the feud, though. It just went on and on. Damned near happened again to others in the families. Several people got creased before it finally died down."

Chapter III

TENDERFOOT AND OUTLAW

A FEW MILES SOUTH of Carson Hole you come to the Divide
Forks campground (née Mudholes) where you may pitch
tent and tarry for up to two weeks. At this and other
campgrounds along the Divide Road you may or may not be
required to put money in the charge box, depending on how
the Forest Service has apportioned the housekeeping
money it has to spend. If camp facilities have been well
maintained this year — firewood cut and ready and all that
good stuff — you pay. If this happens to be a camp they've
had to slight, they don't expect you to pay. They remove the
money box to let you know it.

The kind of people who are willing to put up with
bumpy, dusty roads to explore little-toured country far from
freeway traffic are usually the kind of people who like to
leave the scenery no worse than they found it. You'll notice
very little trash and vandalism up here, even in those
campgrounds the Forest Service has had to neglect for a
time.

At the Forks the Uranium Road (improved graded gravel)
branches to the right, heading down the west side of the
plateau and ending like a frayed-end rope in an incredible
tangle of crooked (and mostly no-good) roads, each leading
to a hole in the ground that is either a mine or what some
prospector fervently hoped would be a mine.

Many of these roads were once-over-lightly passages
scraped off by wandering government bulldozers during the
uranium boom decades ago when the clanking crawlers
roved everywhere at the least scent of radiation, leaving
snail-trail slicks that today are merely sagey scars. At that

Morning sun lays a filagree of shadow across the ochre sand of the Divide Road beyond Carson Hole Narrows.

time a great jagged triangle of rugged country between here and the Dolores River was mapped off as a U.S. Atomic Energy Reserve.

Mining and use of radioactive earth predates the atomic bomb by more years than most people realize. Those mines were going strong in the early years of World War I, as indicated by a newspaper item attacking government intervention (so what else is new?) on January 9, 1914. The article also gives a clue to who was using uranium then, if not for what.

"The declared intention of the Secretary of the Interior to have Congress withdraw mineral land containing carnotite ore does not meet the approval of Western Slope people. It looks too much like a government 'corner.'

"The fact is our miners can supply radium better than can the government if they were given a little encouragement. . . . What the government should do is establish separating and refining plants here so our miners could have a market for their ores nearer than Germany and France."

That vast bowl of rough country down there is threaded with strata color — pretty and promisory as rainbows. The gray purples and gray greens of uranium-bearing Morrison layer . . . the blues of copper outcrops, naming Blue Mesa, Blue Creek and Blue Mud Springs . . . the shrill, day-glow color of carnotite, naming Yellowbird. . . .

Early prospecting by burro and pick has passed to jeep and Geiger counter. After two booms and busts in its almost century-old history, mining in the Tenderfoot Mesa country is prospering again, as witness the newly restored and well-traveled Uranium Road.

Ore that formerly came out over the top on this road to be milled near Grand Junction is now being trucked over the Pine Mountain Road, down literally named S.O.B. Hill to Colorado Highway 141, back through Unaweep Canyon to the uranium mill you saw on the side of the slope as you entered the east end of Unaweep.

Other evocative mine names at the ends of those frayed roads describe attendant hopes and hazards — Climax, Stormy Treasure, Small Spot, Maverick, and Calamity.

Mining and government men, impatient at the creeping progress of wheels over that kind of surface and immensity, took to wings and cleared at least two airstrips, one on Arrowhead and the other on Blue Mesa.

Many features of Uncompahgre geography are named for successful or at least stubbornly persevering cattlemen — Casto Reservoir, Kelso Point, Dillard Mesa, Beach Creek, and many others you will get to know as we go along, from your map, from signboards along the road, and from anecdotes they told or their kids are still telling.

Tenderfoot Mesa, on the contrary, is named for outstanding ineptitude in the *modus operandi* of cowpunching. Cliff-hung above the Dolores River, about as far west as this mountain can claim footing, Tenderfoot is separated from you by a lot of excruciating difficulties such as the breaks of Bull and Maverick canyons.

Just whose gaucheries were responsible for naming that particular mesa seems to be lost to history, but J. D. Dillard, in giving us the flavor of the old roundup days, sort of eases into a story that describes the kind of thing that might have done it:

"Every year at roundup it was always interesting to be settin' around the fire and watchin' 'em come in. Seein' how many of the old faces would be there. A lot were cowpunchers working for the roundup outfits, and they'd change around a lot. A fellow'd be there a year or two and he'd be gone, someone else in this place. Drifters. Now you see 'em, now you don't. We called 'em spooks.

"You could most always tell a new man when he came in, what part of the country he was from. You could tell by his riggin' and the way he handled his horse and all, whether he was from Arizona, Wyoming, Montana, Colorado, Utah — wherever.

"You could also tell without any trouble those that was from countries where cattle were all pretty tame. They'd have three-quarter-rig saddles, and those that didn't wouldn't have a flank cinch. Didn't need one. With wild cattle it's different. You get several hundred pounds of wild cow thrashing around at the end of the rope, and it can take

Sculpture in dead juniper and living stone. Almost any stop along the Divide Road yields treasure for the camera.

more than one strap to keep the saddle from rippin' loose
and goin' with her.

"I'll never forget over at Cross Camp, fellow came in
there from Lone Cone. The Pitchfork Outfit sent him, and
he had a brand-new flank cinch. The rest of his riggin' was
fairly old.

"Ed Maupin and I was standin' there watchin' him un-
saddle and throw off his bed, and it just run through my
mind why he had such a brand new flank cinch riggin'. I
was guessin' to myself he was a new man in the country and
had decided he better conform with the rest of 'em
regardin' the number of straps holdin' saddle and horse together.

"Well, he clean forgot the flank, just undone the front
cinch and jerked the saddle down. Course it turned under
that old pony's belly, and he bogged his head and went to
runnin' and kickin' and buckin' till he got it kicked off.
Didn't hurt anything much, but the fellow was pretty em-
barrassed. Probably forty men was settin' around watchin'
the performance, and he didn't know a soul.

"He took it pretty good. Said, 'Well, hell, I come from a
country where the cattle and the cowboys is gentle. Hadn't
been workin' over there for Lavender very long, and the
boys there at the Cone told me I better put a flank cinch on,
that when I got over here I wouldn't see anything but flank
cinches, and if I didn't they'd know I never worked in rough
country. I guess you know.'"

Early cattlemen, sheepmen, and ore-seekers didn't have
it easy, and they registered some of their troubles in the
names they gave the places where trouble happened. In addition to Hungry Gulch there is Calamity Mesa, Dead Horse
Pasture, Last Dollar Mountain, Starvation Point, and even
The Tongue of Starvation.

The specific disasters these names memorialize have
largely been forgotten, but a few people still remember that
Calamity Mesa got its name when a prospector's burro ate
all his grub, stranding him a good four breakfasts by foot
from the nearest corner grocery. It was probably little com-

fort that one of the rocky humps on his horizon was named Potato Mountain.

In the middle of all that turbulent real estate is Outlaw Mesa, named for John Foster, not exactly because he killed a man — which he did, a man "that needed killing," as he tells it:

"A drifter, Axel Peterson was. And mean. Meaner when drunk. Favorite sport was to ride past the schoolhouse as the kids was getting out, and shoot around their feet just to see 'em jump. Started putting bullets through my cabin one day, with my new wife in it and liable to get killed, so I shot the top of his head off."

This deed was regarded as a public benefaction that nobody else had had the courage to perform and resulted in nothing but good for Foster — the court in Grand Junction paid him and his wife two dollars for their testimony, and the neighbors bought him a new suit of clothes in gratitude — until one day many years later when a mine claim jumper accused *him* of claim jumping, and the prosecution's witness harked back to the shooting by identifying Foster as "that outlaw from the mesa." The name stuck to both mesa and man.

After the Uranium Road drops down off Massey Bench it winds along in the shadow of Leonard Ridge that, with Leonard Basin on the opposite side of the mountain, is the sole remnant of one man's fame. Before map makers froze nomenclature forever up there, this entire mountain was known as Leonard Mesa. Wes Massey remembers this and a little about the man but not his first name.

"Came in here from Boston. Hung that fancy accent on some real basic corral cussing without weakening it any. Brought in a big bunch of shorthorns, unloaded at Dominguez when the Denver & Rio Grande end-of-track got that far between Delta and Grand Junction. Forded his cows across the river and headquartered over here on Blue Creek."

Heading down Indian Creek, the Uranium Road follows (but in this case has not wiped out) one of the plateau's numerous Ute trails that led from good wintering country down on lower benches and river valleys, along both sides of the crest, and up to good summering and hunting country on top.

Many of these trails were segments of a vast network connecting remote but regularly visited places where the seasonal and social activities of this very mobile life-style were conducted — to the plains and buffalo, to the south and trade with the Pueblos (who stayed in one place and thus accumulated things to trade), to the yampa-root harvest in the north, to pow-wow fun and games (mostly gambling) at scores of traditional sites.

Among several of the latter on the plateau is a racetrack on Round Mountain, reached by a still discernable trail up Tabeguache Canyon and 47 Creek to the northeast flank of the mountain where a large cave provided emergency shelter, saving the trouble of building brush wickiups. This cave is also said to have been used by outlaws in later years.

Utes are serious about their racetracks. Plowing up the White River racetrack was the final barbarism that triggered the Meeker Massacre.

It is safe to say that most of the roads now crossing the plateau from one side to the other were laid out along (and thereby obliterated) Indian trails, since these people had thousands of years in which to discover the easiest routes.

We tend to think of Indian trails as tribal secrets traceable only by certain cabalistic signs — a purposely deformed tree branch or riddle figures scratched on a rock. Actually many had been so long and heavily trafficked they were more like narrow roadways, especially after the Indian got the horse and began hauling his possessions, including the heavy leather of his tepee, tied to dragging travois poles.

From centuries of use these trails became almost indelible in the soil. Chet Beal says the place where the Uncompahgre-to-Elk Mountains trail crossed his father's fields on California Mesa near Delta was clearly marked in stunted corn even after seventy years of plowing.

It was probably by following one of these trails that the first alien, a white explorer, set foot on the plateau. Nothing is known about him except that he was a Spaniard looking

Some trees forget what happens to them in childhood, but aspens keep on nagging about it for life.

for gold. That was in 1761 — if you like a thread of dates to hang your mental pictures on — one year after King George III began to flex his tax muscles, resulting in the original Proposition 13 by the thirteen original colonies.

This unknown explorer was followed in four years by Don Juan Maria de Rivera and party under orders from the governor of New Mexico, which was then an immense Spanish territory taking in the Uncompahgre along with the southwest quarter of the continent.

Starting from the east, somewhere near the already ancient town of Santa Fe, he circled into the drainages of the Uncompahgre and Gunnison rivers from the west, over the smooth-looking ridge of the plateau, bypassing the obviously formidable barriers of the Elk Mountains and the San Juans. In so doing he bypassed all the gold; a similarly logical error was undoubtedly what lost his predecessor's name to history.

After crossing the plateau and passing down the Uncompahgre Valley, Rivera made his farthest-north camp at a shallow ford in a mile-wide grassy valley where the Uncompahgre and Gunnison rivers meet, just below the present site of Delta. He saw to it that his name would make the history books by carving it, or at least his initials, the date, and a cross on the trunk of a cottonwood tree.

Ten years after Rivera, more Spaniards were camping at the same ford. This was a small party under Mora and Sandoval, explorers under private not governmental auspices.

A "party" usually consisted (with some doubling in brass) of men to herd the walking meat supply, various scientists of the day such as mappers, miners (at least able to recognize gold when they stumbled over it), agronomists to tell from what grew on the ground whether it was good for farming, ranching, or nothing; mule skinners to nursemaid the pack animals; some kind of a fixer-upper to keep the gear mended and the horses shod; somebody to keep a journal of the trip (in cases where the leaders couldn't read or write, an incapacity too prevalent to embarrass anybody), and Indian guide-interpreters picked up and dropped off along the way.

The Mora and Sandoval journalist duly verified Rivera's *paso-por-aqui* signboard on the Gunnison.

One year later Fathers Dominguez and Escalante set out from Santa Fe with a very large party, to search for a northern route to California that, it was hoped, would pass through friendlier tribes than those who made the southern route frequently fatal. The fathers were also looking for suitable places to found Indian farming settlements and missions.

Dominguez and Escalante considerately picked a date very easy for us to remember, July 4, 1776.

By that time the Uncompahgre was pretty well known to the Spanish; there was no reason to get lost, but they did. For one thing, in their great swing around the west end of the San Juans they hadn't seen a single Indian to ask directions of. The Indians, it later developed, were not hiding, they were up in the mountains gathering berries to make pemican. For another thing, this party included a navigator who apparently placed too much confidence in his equipment — a real-life nautical astrolabe with which he shot the stars every clear night to tell exactly where they were.

They were, it turns out, down in the bottom of the Dolores Canyon, exhaustedly fighting their way through its brush-choked twistings and turnings and forced to cross the stream every three hundred yards or so. Dolores, a Spanish word for pain and grief, understates their predicament.

They'd got themselves into this fix on the toss of a coin.

The navigator had wanted to go straight west and put the Sierra behind before snow shut down. The fathers, whose organization had had no luck whatever in taming nomadic Indians to the business end of plow and irrigation shovel, had heard of some Utes to the northeast who might be induced to settle down and work like the Pueblos — not taking into account the fact that each different life-style had had a thousand years to become ingrained.

A lot was riding on the toss. Up to now they had been more or less following the Ute slave-trade trail — the trail used by Utes to take young Digger Indians, captured in Montana, to Santa Fe to trade them for horses.

The navigator lost the toss.

Extricating them from the Dolores, he took them up the side of the Uncompahgre, over terrain so rough the horses and cattle (after all that soaking in the river) left bloody tracks on the rocks. Eventually they discovered the easy going of an Indian trail that, unnoticed, had been running alongside them all the way. About the same time the first Indian appeared — a Tabeguache Ute who guided them over the Hill.

The cavalcade sidestepped the ford at the confluence of the Uncompahgre and Gunnison rivers, cutting across the adobe badlands between what are now Olathe and Austin. Somebody from the party must have ridden down to the ford, because Escalante records that Rivera's signpost still existed.

Incidentally, though two of the enormous clefts that pierce the Uncompahgre Plateau were named for the two Spanish priests — Dominguez and Escalante canyons — neither of the men ever set foot in the beautiful canyons that many years later would be named for them.

Chapter IV

COWBOY PLACE NAMES

WHEN YOU WERE at Carson Hole Narrows you were looking out on both sides of the divide at once, but what you saw was a canyon's opposite wall. A few miles farther on — where signs point to Massey Cowcamp — you come out on a high, open saddle where you can sight your camera on Grand Mesa to the east and swing in your tracks to photograph the La Sal Mountains in Utah to the west.

Variations on this grand view across immense valley to distant mountains on both sides at once will happen a number of times before you leave this skyline ridge. In some of them your line of sight follows the back-slant of the plateau all the way to where the cap rock (still Dakota sandstone) dives under Grand Mesa. Though the Uncompahgre lacks little more than a thousand feet of being as tall as Grand Mesa, the youngest (highest) rocks on the plateau are older than the oldest (bottom) rocks of Grand Mesa.

Another of these saddle views occurs where Mailbox Branch and Smith Creek head up in meadows on opposite sides of the Divide Road.

Here you are in a region of mountaintop springs, a fact noted in the naming of the Cold Springs Ranger Station down a road to the left just beyond the view saddle. One spring is so close to the road you will probably be stared at by cows and calves that have tanked up on water till they look too dazed to walk six steps toward grass.

Another spring oozes from the ground just past Bug Point. (That bulge in the scenery to the right, across from the road to the ranger station, is Bug Point.) This spring is at the head of another branch, Bunch Ground Branch, a name

View into Utah from a saddle of the Uncompahgre crest. Salt basins lie hidden this side of skyline mountains.

that probably explains the naming of Bug Point — you gather several thousand cattle together on a bunch ground, and there's bound to be a congregation of flies, gnats, and mosquitos following their natural food supply.

Mailbox Branch marks an early-day communications device that had nothing to do with the U. S. Post Office Department, which (with two exceptions, one in Escalante Canyon and the other along the narrow-guage railroad over Dallas Divide) pretended the Uncompahgre Plateau and its scattered population did not exist.

At Mailbox Branch a wooden box was fastened to a post. Whoever passed was supposed to look inside to see whether anyone had left a letter to be mailed in town or to be hand-delivered any convenient distance this side. Anybody coming from town deposited in the box whatever mail there was for folks in the immediate area.

Desperation shopping lists also could be filled this way. Critically out of lard or a replacement for a broken kingpin? You could rely on any townbound passerby to get the item for you, put it in the box, and wait for repayment at the next chance meeting.

This delivery system, beginning with saddle and pack-horse, continued through wagon, Model T, and pickup truck eras. It hasn't been all that long since the box was used. Though down off the post it is still there, hidden in sage and grass.

Along the length of the Divide Road signs point to cow camps on both sides, but usually well down from the top. This is not because the road was laid out to avoid them or because cattlemen were paranoic about company — quite the contrary! — but because the cow camps were situated at springs, and springs rarely occur on the crest of mountains, which in the singular case of the plateau happened to be the easiest place to lay out a lengthwise road. Equally singular, this mountain does have at least half a dozen springs right on the crest, such as the area where you are now.

The high-country camps were summer residences for the ranch families, and several of them still are. In pre-auto days, when it took a long time to ride and pack to the spot where the summer business of cud-harvesting mountain grass was going on, these high camps placed the stockmen handy to cows that might get into trouble from bogs, dried up waterholes, poison larkspur, disease, or general cussedness.

At first winter quarters were more elaborate cabins situated down in sun-pocket canyon bottoms or lower mesa benches near winter grazing or haying grounds. Later the ranchers, or at least their families, wintered in town houses. Old-timer Wes Massey explains:

"Most of the early settlers were bachelors, stockmen, and prospectors, and they stayed that way, figuring if they got married they'd have to move to town to put the kids in school. When one of them did get hitched, the others mourned like it was a death. 'Give him six year, then he'll leave the range.'

"Calhoun got married. People said, 'In six years you'll have to have a school.' Calhoun bought the Club outfit in 1906, ran it to 1919, and left for school. Schooling ran them into town. In 1920 the gals got the vote, and the Model T came along. They all went to town and never did come back. Them old ranch gals got out of the wilderness and all that hard work, and they put their kids in school so they wouldn't have to live that life. Completely unfitted 'em for ranching by making doctors and lawyers of 'em."

A number of Delta and Grand Junction citizens were born up here on the plateau, some without benefit of physician. Usually a neighbor woman with some midwife experience was called in, but up here where every man had plenty of practice bringing life into the world the natural way, there was nothing new or cultish about a husband sharing the birth experience with his wife.

Ironically, the cow camp isolation, considered such a handicap in pioneer days, is now cherished as an unmatched opportunity to get away from the pressures of modern life into simplicity, peace, and quiet — of course slightly soured by the above-listed bovine predicaments and innate cussedness.

Never straight for long, the Divide Road curves into everchanging vistas such as this sidelong spotlight of evening sun.

J. D. Dillard was born on the lower fringe of the plateau. He says he remembers it well.

"It was May 3, 1899, in winter cow camp on the Roubideau. One of those late storms — May storm, real bad one. I lay there on that bed and watched those cattle trailin' by all day long, and it started me worryin' about cattle havin' enough feed, and I have continued to worry about just such a thing ever since."

Dillard enlarges on his early introduction into self-reliance: "When I was six weeks old the family moved to summer camp, and they made me carry my own bedroll."

The cow camp signs along the road are a roster of early cattlemen — Casto, Craig, Weil, Whiting, Black, Massey, Wadlow, Taylor, Woodring, Holland, Huffington, Musser, Blumberg, Shreeves, Smith, Calhoun, Davis, Love, Dillard, Lockhart, Beach, Maupin . . . names important in Western Slope history and in present-day life.

A few of the early-day cattlemen's names have been lost to the industry but are perpetuated on the map — such as Kelso Point — but many of the original outfits are still in the family down to the fourth generation.

Before these outfits settled into permanent allotments there was a long period of territorial musical chairs. Squatters rights, claim jumping, homesteading for pay, and dealing in pre-emptions were the order of the day. Dillard recalls, "My dad said there's hardly a spring or waterhole on the plateau that wasn't jumped at some time."

A man would cut four logs, rope and snake them into a square indicating he intended to build a cabin there sometime when he got around to it, stake out as much land around his spring as he thought he could get away with, ride off to town for coffee and beans, and come back to find somebody else squatting inside the square, claiming his claim and water source.

But enough claims were pegged down to put more than thirty thousand acres of forest land into private hands.

Big outfits bought, squeezed, or bluffed out smaller ones that couldn't make a go. The Club, pushing in huge herds and hiring aggressive punchers, dominated as much of the plateau as they could, and may have had their eye on the whole thing. At one time Club was branding five thousand calves a year and figuring they weren't getting more than 50 per cent of the calf crop.

The boss's (or anybody's) unbranded stray calves were a walking resource that tempted some cowboys, discontent with their "$30 and found" monthly pay, to earmark them (literally) with brands of their own, thus adding to the number of outfits grazing the Hill.

The U-C (Utah-Colorado Cattle Company) was running about three thousand cows and bringing in another three thousand Utah steers every year to fatten on plateau grass. Club and U-C alone ran almost twice the number of head now permitted to graze on the entire plateau, and there were many more cattle companies, as you will note by the cow-camp signboards along the road. Within twenty years of the time of first herds came in from Texas, Kansas, Mexico, and other points east and south, the town of Placerville on the San Miguel had become the largest cattle-shipping point in the world. The cow outfits were eating the mountain right down to the nub.

Cattle companies were named for brands as well as owners — the Club, for instance, took its name from the ace of clubs branded on Club cattle. The 7-N, the Lazy Y, the 41, the Dot, the U-C, signified not only brand but company. Some outfits ran several brands. Dillard's father, Jeff, was hired by the San Miguel Cattle Company (later the Club) to bring in the first three thousand head of Texas cattle because he could recognize the thirty road-brands involved.

The Dot cow camp, off to your left as your car tops the next rise in the road, is an illustration of some of the difficulties when brands were first registered. It was considerably easier to plunk a hot iron on a critter than to try to describe the shape of the resulting tattoo in words. The Dot brand reads: "Circle dot with a swing L over the hips."

The Dot was started by Bert Enore, known as "the lucky little Englishman who brought good Nevada horses to the area." Enore also brought in Mexican cows that, perhaps not unlike their human counterparts below the border, produced so dependably they contributed more than their share to the plateau's bovine overpopulation problems.

"Those little Mexican cows were great breeders," Dillard remembers. "Enore'd have a bigger calf crop than almost anybody in the area."

They were also great little joggers, according to Morgan Hendrickson. "They could trot down the road for miles. You didn't dare holler at them; they'd just leave the country. When Maupin took his cows off the mountain they'd get into a trot and keep it up all the way down to Roubideau.

"Those little Mexicans were about as close to racing stock as cows get — except for Brahmas, that can outrun a horse on the short haul. I'll never forget the consternation when the first Brahma bulls came onto the mountain. All the cow horses had to rethink their herding techniques."

One cow outfit took its name from the scenery. The annual shape of snowbanks on the face of the mountain above Nucla, resembling the numerals 4 and 7, are said to be the origin of the 47 brand and 47 Cattle Compnay operating in that area of the Uncompahgre.

The first cattlemen, miners, and loggers moving onto the vacant plateau found themselves with a naming job about as extensive as Adam faced in the Garden of Eden. Some kind of place identification was vital in directing a cowhand to a particular spot where strays had found a new hangout.

Undoubtedly the mountain was already well equipped with Indian place names when the white man arrived. Indians would have found it just as necessary to have mutually understood identifying names for landscape features. If so, the pioneers were oblivious — the map carries only four names of Indian origin: Uncompahgre itself, Unaweep Canyon, Tabeguache Creek and Basin, and Shavano, the name of a creek on the west side of the plateau and of a valley on the east side.

Shavano was a Ute chief along with Captain Jack, Douglas, Colorow, and several others, all on a par with Chief Ouray until the United States, for treaty purposes, elevated Ouray above them. Tabeguache translates something like "Place where snows melt first," describing its sun-facing slopes. It is also the name of the Ute tribe that made the vast bowl its home base.

In addition to their personal and brand names, the early settlers designated places for prevalent flora and fauna. There are Cottonwood and Willow creeks on both sides of the divide, Columbine Pass, Buck Canyon, Sagehen Ridge, Turkey Plot, Coyote Basin, Tarantula Reservoir, and Bear Den Rim. All are mapped places you will come to, or be up-mountain from, as you advance along the crest.

Pieces of scenery were named for horses whose favorite haunt they were. Socks and Dan Mesa is named for a light buggy team that made a beeline for that spot as soon as unhitched. They had to be fetched from there (a good long jaunt) every time the missus wanted to drive to town. Queen's Point was appropriated by, and named for, a thoroughbred mare belonging to Sam Maupin.

Roberts Brothers, first-comers on the plateau, were Kentucky racehorse breeders. Potter Basin, Monitor, and Briggs mesas were named for three of their prize racing stallions who ran bands of mares on their respective territories. Briggs Mesa lost a little class, becoming workaday Sawmill Mesa after Briggs died defending his band from a mountain lion, and Sam Skinner built an early sawmill there.

Some landscape was dubbed according to the degree of difficulty it presented — Good Point and Bad Point, S.O.B. Hill, Rough Draw (a poker hand?), Lightning Basin, Terrible Creek, and the ultimate — Hell's Hole.

Almost any happening could name a place forever. A few that aren't on your map but are known to everybody who rides Plateau cow trails are:

Butcher Knife — near Cross Camp. Got its name when somebody lost one there, somebody else found it and stuck it into a tree so the loser could recover it. He never came back, and the tree has grown over it until now only a bit of the handle shows. But it is a place, A man can say, "Still looking for that brindle-face heifer? Saw her over at Butcher Knife yesterday."

Water Glass — on Kelso Point. Named for the drinking glass kept there on a willow stob by Alex Calhoun after he got too old and stiff to get down and drink from the spring and the customary cowboy fashion, flat on his face.

Dinner Park — at the upper end of Love Mesa. One meal tagged it for all time. "Uncle Bob Stone was moving cattle down off Stone's Bench, came across the top, and they stopped there, unpacked, and cooked up a bite," Dillard explains. What does a cowboy on the move cook up? Well, beef of course (they butchered again whenever they ran out) with sourbough bread and beans if they'd loaded the pack animal with the conveniences, skillet-fried if not. Ted Lockhart says Dinner Park became a regular chuck wagon stop on the roundup.

Karo Hill — on Brushy Ridge. Got its name when the Lockhart family was moving up to summer camp one year. The four kids were driving the cavy of saddle horses, mother and dad were up in the wagon that was loaded with bedding and groceries enough to last till fall.

"The wagon jounced over an extra big rock, and the two Karo syrup buckets rolled out and busted open on the road before our eyes," Ted Lockhart relates, anguish still tinging his voice. "We just watched our whole summer's sweetness sink into the dirt."

It is against the grain of probabilities that the same accident could have happened to the same brand of sweetener at exactly the same place, but the difficulty of establishing the facts long after the event is pointed up by a second explanation for Karo Hill.

Morgan Hendrickson admits he got his story secondhand, but he stands by his source. Bill Blumberg is the victim in this version.

"Bill was returning from town to the Blumberg cow camp with a bucket of syrup among the groceries on his packhorses. The lid jiggled loose and left a sticky trail all the way up the hill. Bill was famous for being tight, but there's nothing to the rumor he tried to lick it off the rocks."

Coffee Pot — nobody now living knows where it is, or how it got its name, but many remember there was such a place.

Wagon Park — in the wilderness between Big and Little

Dominguez creeks and on the map. Somebody somehow got a wagon onto this bench over a trail a horseback rider would rather not tackle, despaired of ever getting it back down, and simply walked off and left it to rot.

Sowbelly Ridge — just north of the Escalante, also mapped. Named for an Old Batch, not how he looked but how he lived — on pork saltside and beans.

Ranchers, who had no compunction about laying outlandish names on the geography, extended a like discourtesy to each other, calling and answering to such names as Preach Massey, Punch Holland, Pink Blumberg, Wash Hocker, and Wind River. One man is still inexplicably referred to as Bud No Name.

Curiously, in designating spots on the plateau, the owner and what he owned became fused into a kind of name-place-entity. A simple farm or ranch that in other localities would always be spoken of as a possession — "I'm riding over to McHugh's [place] today" — becomes itself a place. A man says, "I'm going to McHugh," the way he would say, "I'm going to Grand Junction," even though McHugh (between the cliffs and the Gunnison River) was never more than a homesteader's ranch that has since been owned by other people with other names. Sawtell is another old-timer who became place rather than person.

Locations where horse thieves have been caught and hanged have resulted in Horse Thief creeks and Horse Thief canyons all over Western maps. The crime of the Uncompahgre Plateau's culprit (at least the one they caught and remember) was less common than his color, so the place where they killed and buried him under a pile of rocks was named Nigger Gulch.

Oscar Huffington recorded the event that "happened when I was a kid going to school." The man stole a horse off Delta Main Street and was trying to get out of the country. Sheriff Ben Gheen tracked the horse nearly out to Escalante and found it grazing, no rider, no one around. He started back to return the horse when the thief stepped out from a rock yelling, "Where're you going with my horse!" The sheriff attempted to take him in, too, but the man began throwing rocks at him. When the sheriff shot over his head, the man only threw more rocks. "So the sheriff had to kill him."

Later, sociologically cleaned up, the place was remapped Negro Gulch. It runs into the Gunnison a few miles west of Delta.

Speaking of cleaning up the map, one spot has been cleaned clear off. J. D. Dillard tells the story:

Long after the Indians had been moved into Utah they returned each year to habitual hunting grounds on the plateau to kill and cure their winter supply of deer jerky. Like some modern hunters they occasionally had trouble distinguishing between deer and fat steers down the rifle sights.

When this had happened a little too often to be put down to accident, the cowmen called a meeting in one of the plateau glades to straighten them out on the difference between the species. The pow-wow (Dillard calls it a chingrow) lasted all day, and at the end of it both sides retired to the bordering bushes to drop their pants and answer the call of nature.

The park became known far and wide by the day's concluding activity. But when Forest Service cartographers got around to mapping the plateau they felt obliged to change it from a four to a five-letter word, rechristening it Nasty Park.

Apparently even that was too much. If you have a recent map you will find Nasty Park missing.

Chapter V

ROBBERS' TRAIL

A MILE OR SO beyond Bug Point the McCarty Trail comes
out on the Divide Road from the east in one of the crest's
largest and loveliest saddles. You won't find the trail marked
that way; it is now called Brushy Ridge Trail in its upper
reaches. This is the trail the McCarty Gang took, old-timers
say, coming and going on their way to relieve the Delta
Farmers and Merchants Bank of some of its cash in 1893.

The map-charted part of the McCarty Trail leaves Escalante Creek not far from the canyon mouth, climbs to
McCarty Bench, and follows Camp Ridge to join what is
now Brushy Ridge Trail at a point where the latter wriggles
steeply out of the North Fork of the Escalante.

The McCarty Trail is another instance of the plateau's
predilection for coincidence and paradox. The McCarty
Gang used it only once — but so notoriously that it is generally believed to be named for them. In reality it was
McCarty Trail long before they ever saw it, named for Justin
McCarty who winter-fed Ouray mine mules there and used
the trail to get them up to spring grass.

Just which of many possible trails the robbers took in
coming up the west side of the mountain a lot of people
have tried to discover. The men left several thousand dollars
of "mad money" stashed there, probably all in gold coin,
the leavings from former bank robberies in Telluride, Denver, Oregon, and so on. No one has ever claimed to have
found it.

The place is somewhere in the Tabeguache Basin. If you
can position yourself on this saddle so you look down over

the shoulder of the mountain straight south, you will be looking at it. Yes, indeed, that is a lot of country!

Most of the digging has been done in a north-heading spur of Tabeguache Canyon known as Robber's Roost. It is a cave-pocked area not far from the Ute racetrack — and from Starvation Point!

In late summer 1893 the brothers Tom and Bill McCarty and Bill's 20-year-old son Fred were "holed up in a horse thieves' hangout on the Tabeguache," making preparations for the Delta operation. The older men were dragging their feet because the installation of the telegraph in frontier towns was making horseback holdups and getaways increasingly risky; but young Fred, who had never been in on a robbery and desperately wanted to be, pressured his elders. Caleb Casebier gives details:

"Before departing, they wrapped a pair of saddlebags in oilskin and buried them in dry soil not far from the creek. The bags contained over $3,000. The hiding place was well marked so that anyone of the three could retrieve it.

"Caching their money was an act the McCarty's always performed before going on a raid. They recognized the fact that all three might not ride back. The money would be there for the survivors."

Only one rode back, and he was running for his life, with no time to swing wide for the money.

After crossing the plateau at dawn, the gang stationed relay mounts near the head of Maverick and rode to Delta on their best horseflesh, racing stock said to be the fastest in the area. Of these the best was a white horse, Suze, belonging to Tom, who had a weakness for fast white horses and equally fast blonde women.

Customary *modus operandi* for banks jobs required three men — two to do the job and a third to hold the getaway horses in the nearest alley. Normally the third man was the least experienced, but young Fred yearned to be in on the action, so it was Tom, old hand and mentor of Butch Cassidy, who waited while Fred and his father entered the bank and pulled guns on the two cashiers.

Cashier Blatchley was too startled or too heroic to turn

over the money quietly. Stories differ as to whether he
yelled, reached for a gun, or both. At any rate, young
McCarty lost his cool and shot him. Or perhaps he had been
self-psyched to do it all along.

With murder on their hands, the robbers were now more
interested in getting away than in getting away with money.
The bag of gold coins Fred did manage to scoop up fell from
his hands as the man grabbed leather and raced out of town.

Hardware dealer Simpson brought two of them down
with a Sharps rifle. Tom McCarty on Suze outrode pursuers
and made it up the McCarty trail to the relay mounts, where
he turned Suze loose to find his own way home. Don Musser saw the outlaw in flight, but until he heard about the
bank robbery later, he didn't know the kind of history he
was looking at.

Tom McCarty found a hidey-hole on Fill 'em Up Mesa in
the La Sal Mountains outlaw country; he stayed low for a
while then slipped away to the Pacific Northwest and never
came back.

While at the La Sal rendezvous he must have disclosed
the whereabouts of the Tabeguache gold cache to somebody, because during the Great Depression another relative,
Ekky McCarty, had a map showing where the treasure is.
He never found it.

The Divide Road saddle at this point has as its pommel a
ridge culminating in Uncompahgre Butte, an unspectacular
hump three hundred feet above the road. It does, however,
offer spectacular views in all directions.

Its gentle, oval dome seems too nonmomentous to have
a name at all, much less two. Also called Montpelier, it is
9,679 feet above sea level, not the highest point on this road
by any means. A jeep road circles from the south to the top.

Nice little walk.

If you choose not to make the climb, never mind; there is
another saddle just beyond, providing one more of the
plateau's windows on infinity.

The picturesque pole-worm drift fences that meander so
photogenically across glades and into forests in these open

At Monument the top-of-the-world feeling — that you are helping hold up the sky — is eased by the intimate curves of a little side road.

places are not antique remnants of pioneer ranching days or nostalgia-catering anachronisms put up to make the forest prettier. They are working equipment, built and kept up by joint efforts of the Forest Service and permitees, the latter as part of their per-head pasture fee on government land.

Drift fences keep cows in their place. One continuous fence runs the entire length of the plateau, segregating east from west.

"Before that fence went in," Morgan Hendrickson says, "you'd have cattle from any place on the plateau eating your grass, licking your salt, drinking your springwater, singly or in bunches. Like three old cows from the Tabeguache that thought they belonged on the Escalante. Had to be taken home every roundup, always came back."

Lateral fences (all those cattle guards you've been crossing) zigzag down both sides of the mountain to keep cows in their allotments and their owners out of trouble over grazing permits.

In the old days there were other lengthwise fences farther down called "poison fences," put up to hold the cattle on lower ranges in the spring when the high-country larkspur was at its deadliest. After this danger had passed it was an early summer chore to ride the fence, letting down the bars so the cows could graze on up to the top.

Wooden fences are economical. In this day of the chain saw, and with aspens near and abundant, it is cheaper and quicker to lay up a pole-worm fence than to dig postholes for stringing wire, especially over terrain where the natural paving of sandstone is frequently covered by only a few inches of soil, if at all. Some of this work is done by crews from the Roubideau Honor Camp down at the bottom of the hill.

"Worm fence is better for deer," a ranger points out, "Running at full speed in the forest, deer can spot the pole fence in time to leap over. With barbed wire they can get tangled and cut before they know it's there. We do have to make sure the spaces between the lower poles are large enough to allow small fawns to slip through where their

Wild flowers froth through pewter gray fence. The gap enables fawns to slip through and follow the leaping mother deer.

mothers have leaped over, otherwise babies may be left behind as the band moves on."

A large billboard-type sign beside the road brings other range and forest improvements to your attention. Terrace ditching across steep slopes slows rain and snowmelt runoff, reduces erosion, and increases the yield of grass. A system of catch ponds scattered over the plateau puts the drinking water out where the grass is, spreads the cattle, and reduces overgrazing near the infrequent natural springs.

Those treeless patches you see down on the distant mesas below the forest line are not natural either.

The 1930s Taylor Grazing Act, fathering the Bureau of Land Management, extended government regulation into nontimber forests of juniper and pinyon. These trees provided Indians and prehistoric peoples with scores of vital products (pinyon nuts for food, soft inner bark of junipers for papoose diapers, to name only two) but were used by white men only for firewood and fence posts, neither of which was deemed as necessary to later economy as cow and deer feed. So they were chained off. Two huge tractors pulling a heavy chain stretched between them simply mowed the trees down to make way for grass.

These cleared areas, like other government open lands, were then artificially seeded with various grasses and forbs to suit the climatic conditions and the appetites of cattle, sheep, deer, and elk.

There was some difference of opinion about what might appeal to a cow's palate. In fact, there were differences of opinion about almost everything right from the start in this drag-foot government-cattleman partnership.

College-bred foresters tended to scorn the ideas of cattlemen who hadn't even finished grade school — though you had to admit something was going right when a rancher (or his wife, if he were too busy to go to town) could walk into the bank any old day and take out a loan of fifty thousand dollars just on say-so.

Cattlemen tended to snort at the pronouncements of a young squirt over-fed on books in Eastern schools and without a lick of range experience to his name.

Every now and then one of these squirts would do something to prove the ranchers' point. They never let him forget it.

Like the field trip where a range expert was lecturing on the utter unpalatability, inedibility, and proposed eradication of a certain plant — all the while his own horse was avidly eating it down to the roots.

Like the time a zealous ranger, told to put out salt in inaccessible places so the deer and cattle would spread the grazing more evenly, took the instruction literally and placed salt on a cliff accessible only to chipmunks.

If Forest Service personnel had similar put-down stories on its side, they remained in-house jokes in the interests of public relations.

Actually their ideas and work soon began speaking for them, as the mountain started to "come back" and began to contrast favorably with other highlands that were timbered off and grazed off to the point of no return.

About those treeless mesas down there, ringed with junipers — even among government agency men there is difference of opinion as to the advisibility of tree-chaining; in fact, the operation has slowed almost to a complete stop in recent years. Perhaps they, too, are coming back; with binoculars you can see small new trees twinkling all over those mesas among the bland grasses.

All is regulated now on public lands. Open and closed grazing dates are firm. Cows may not come onto the forest until the grass has a certain head start, and grazing may not continue so late in the fall that there is no top growth left to mat and protect the roots.

Wild game, once living as random and chancy as birdflight, is now all accounted for. An estimated eighteen thousand deer, twenty-four hundred elk, and nearly eighteen thousand head of domestic livestock may feed without damage to the herbage of this mountain. Any overage of game is "harvested" in hunting season. Also listed in the Uncompahgre Plateau wild game tally are 310 black bear, 10 mountain lions, and 50 wild turkeys.

At one time bighorn sheep grazed here — Eddie Jones

Contour ridges retard snowmelt runoff, promoting thicker grass and forbs for cattle, deer, and elk.

found a skull with curling horns intact not too long ago. Their sudden and complete disappearance is said to have been caused not by overhunting but by diseases introduced by domestic sheep, against which they had no natural immunity or defense.

The entire mountain was suffering disease unto death. Many of the huge cattle companies were absentee owners (Eastern or English) who paid no taxes or fees and had no interest in orderly development. They mined grass the way they mined gold veins — to get it all and get out.

Cattle population pressures made regulation necessary to save the range. Now, people population pressures are inevitably necessitating ever more and more regulation.

You may not gather flagstone from desert BLM lands without a permit. You may not gather deadwood in the forest for your fireplace, cut a Christmas tree, or dig a yucca for your yard without a permit. In most cases, unless for commercial purposes, the permits are free, but they are required.

"We have to know what people are doing, how much, and where," a BLM manager explains. "Moss rock, for instance, that takes decades or even centuries to form, could entirely disappear in a short time."

How stringent and well-patrolled such regulations can be, at least farther west, is cited by an Uncompahgre rockhound after a trip to the Southwest.

"Just stoop over to tie your shoe, and some official spy in plain clothes (jeans, backpack, and beard) pops up from behind a rock and accuses you of illegally picking up one of the 'the peoples' arrowheads!' "

With the government so firmly in control now, it is hard to imagine what it was like when the power was all on the other side.

Cowmen who built up the first big-capital cattle empires did so by sheer drive, guts to take chances, fierce individualism, and acquisitiveness.

Up to their necks in denim and dirty work, they nevertheless were barons. Their swashbuckling hats, the horses they rode, and the saddles they sat were the best money could buy — working gear but also status symbols.

They could toil and sweat together at roundups, help each other in trouble, drink and joke together, but they could not cease being rivals. Outfits were programmed to get bigger, and this could only happen at the expense of neighbor and grass. Even though they knew their unrestricted expansion was destroying their basic working capital, the graze, they couldn't change. It was open range; if stockman Jones reduced his herd to let the grass come back, stockman Smith's cows would drift in and chew off what he saved.

It was the little outfits, they say, that called in a governmental arbiter, petitioning that the plateau become federal land. President Teddy Roosevelt created the Uncompahgre National Forest in 1905.

Unable to regulate themselves from within the associations, the cattlemen knew they needed an outside referee, but they didn't have to like him — especially when he was a kid not long out of school, wearing a Boy Scout hat and frog pants, and sitting on a McClellan saddle.

A forester in those early days wrote plaintively in his report:

"Can you imagine how I feel in a group of cowmen all sitting lordly on the most expensive Western riding equipment, and me on a McClellan saddle?"

The McClellan saddle, army, was minimal riding tack about the size of the scorned English pancake saddle but without class. No spare leather anywhere. You could chafe the skin off the inside of your knees on unfendered rings and buckles. No leather was wasted covering the two sides of the saddletree; the gap was simply left open right down to the bare horse. Somewhat like riding a galloping potty chair.

From this low-totem position the Forest Service began very slow, tactful, and tentative relations with the cattlemen, reducing herds by a few cows here, a few there, applauding cooperation when they found it, ignoring (but recording) resistance and violations. They strove to be one of the boys —

at a meeting devoted to ideas on bettering the Service and getting along with cattlemen, one ranger asked earnestly, "Should a ranger be a good poker player?"

Immediately they set about trying to bring the range back, testing numerous grasses to find one that would thrive in the often arid Western Slope climate, be palatable to animals, and put fast poundage on young steers. They spent a great deal of time, brains, and taxpayers' money experimenting with scores of grass varieties. At one point they hoped to make the plateau another bluegrass country, but it froze out, burned out, or something. Finally they found just the right one — Indian rice grass.

It was growing here all the time.

This was not the governmental boondoggle it appears to be. The original Indian rice grass, being a favorite with animals, had been all but wiped out during the overgrazing.

Chapter VI

UNCOMPAHGRE BASEMENT DOOR

UNCOMPAHGRE BUTTE is the signal that you are passing, on your left, a cross-mountain watershed from the drainage of Dominguez Canyon to that of Escalante Canyon. It isn't much of a divide; these two streams and all their tributaries are cut almost parallel to each other down the east slope of the mountain but are separated by a subdivide that sidles from the butte to Snipe Mountain and runs down the finger of Bruṣhy Ridge.

The ridge makes an attempt to provide you with some kind of roadable grade on which to coast all the way down to the Gunnison River, as 25 Mesa does farther on, but it gives up in a welter of stringy mesas and arroyos all bent on pursuing independent courses and not being dragged into the drainages of the big boys on either side.

Indeed there are signs that the Little Dominguez also once went its own way, emptying directly into the river. There are only two hundred feet and a little over a mile preventing that pre-reunion now — a mere nothing in this gouged-out country — but apparently Big Dominguez cut faster and stole the water from Little brother (sounds like one of those shovel feuds prevalent in early days when irrigation water was being nailed down on the Western Slope) forcing it to make a right angle turn and become a mere tributary for its last half mile.

All along, from Uncompahgre Butte to just north of Columbine Pass, the headwater tendrils of the Escalante system touch the Divide Road, like the top twigs of a pruned-flat tree, causing most of the ups and downs and curves that compose perfection for your camera. Escalante is the only stream on the entire mountain that conforms in any way to the normal "branching tree" shape so familiar on maps of rivers. It does so grudgingly, its branches joining the mainstream trunk at tight, almost parallel angles, rather resembling the bottom of a Lombardy popular.

This gathering of streams into the trunk leaves the intervening mesas cliff-hung, high and dry, with the resulting "points" so much a feature of this part of the mountain. There is Short Point, Long Point, Good Point, Bad Point, Middle Point, and a lot of pointy stuff known to cowpunchers unaffectionately as the Escalante Breaks. Carved mainly of red rock, frothed with forest from ponderosa to juniper, they are beautiful.

In the saddleglades along the first part of this stretch, before the woods get too thick, you will be looking down across Escalante land on one side and on the west into a tumbled mess carved out of headlong creeks that get down off the mountain fast, often leaping from ledge to ledge like icing trickling down the layers of a torte.

The masses and clefts within your view have fascinating names. Moon Mesa, Coyote Basin, Bull Draw, Hog Park. (*Hog? Park?*) The biggest thing in sight, cutting straight across your vision about halfway down, is Campbell Point, named for another plateau tragedy. Wes Massey tells the story:

"Two fellows named Jones and Campbell were partners in some mining and ranch property. Campbell got greedy, waylaid Jones on the trail to Gateway, shot him, and packed the body up onto that mesa and dropped it over the edge.

"After a few days Campbell reported Jones missing and joined the neighbors in the search.

"Well, it took about ten days, but they tracked Jones' horse up onto the mesa and found signs where the body was dragged to the rim. It's about a thousand foot drop there, but Jones had landed on a ledge, and the search party could see him.

"They put their lariats together and roped a man down three hundred feet to bring him up. By that time the body was in pretty bad shape, and the bullet that killed him just

What seem slumps of shrubs on the far hill are individual forests. Each forest is a "family," since aspens spread by roots, and every tree is blood cousin to every other in the group.

fell out. Campbell spent ten years in the state pen but got consumption so was freed before his time was up."

On the opposite side of the Divide Road there is even more history. Find a place where you can look out over the drainage of the Escalante, and take a driving break while we enter this mountain by the back door at basement level.

The only car-safe road on the Uncompahgre which is not part of the Divide Road or its accesses is the road into Escalante Canyon bottoms. It is reached by a turnoff on U.S. Highway 50 about ten miles north of Delta.

For its first few hundred yards through dryland sage and shad scale the road slopes gently down, then it crosses an insignificant bridge over an insignificant dry wash and slopes as gently up again for a mile or so.

That shallow valley is the dividing line between the Uncompahgre Plateau and Grand Mesa. Never mind that just over the hill is the drop-off of the Gunnison River Canyon, hundreds of feet deep. It's the river, not the meeting of mountains, that is misplaced. This little valley is it. Here the top layer of the plateau dives under Grand Mesa — tawny Dakota sandstone on the west, gray adobe of Mancos shale on the east. The strange little valley runs mile after mile, all the way from Point Rock near Delta to Whitewater, paralleling mountains, river, and highway all the way. At intervals gullies carrying Grand Mesa runoff (Wells and Beaver gulches, Sectionhouse Draw) plow down through the valley to the river, confusing the issue.

Where the canyon swings deeper into the plateau wide stretches of the lower Uncompahgre are cut off. One of these is the Hunting Ground west of Indian Creek on Highway 50. These stretches provided perfect game traps for the Indian before and after he got the rifle and the horse. Deer browsing in these upland island strips would not break from the shelter of juniper-pinyon cover to cross the scary open country to the east, and in only a few places, such as Deer Creek and Deer Run, could they get down the cliffs.

Women and children, skulking in a line upward from the

flats, would nudge the suspicious bands up through the breaks to the canyon rims where they were cliff-trapped, easy prey from Indian men shooting from blinds.

A few of these blinds are still to be seen on the canyon rims north of the Escalante Road — circles and breastworks of dry-laid, flat rock that later proved to be rich hunting ground for arrowhead collectors.

The Escalante Road bores down to Gunnison River level through a nameless side gulch, scarred on its opposite slope by traces of an earlier access, the Gold Road. It was scraped off during the Great Depression by a group of Grand Junction men who hoped to get rich, or at least postpone starvation, by placering the gold-bearing gravels that form bluffs on the next bench above the canyon bottom here.

They rigged three old car motors to power their sluice jiggler and pump the necessary water up from the river. But the gold was "goosefeather gold," tiny tissue flakes so light they floated right over the sluice riffles.

Escalante Canyon was settled early. Drawn by the year-around stream and the enclosed warmth of red cliffs, squatters staked out claims even before there was any survey line to hang their legal rights on. The nearest benchmark was in Plateau Valley on the far side of Grand Mesa. Envisioning vast possibilities of litigation in court and bloodshed out of court the government hurriedly dispatched a chain crew to spin a single spider-thread survey line up over that turbulent immensity and down across the Gunnison. It didn't arrive intact. Only much later was it discovered that an error had shoved one whole township askew, creating another that is full length on two sides but only a quarter of a mile wide.

A disproportionate number of cattle outfits had their winter quarters in this canyon, contributing a disproportionate share of the mountain's history and anecdote.

It begins at the black iron bridge, which, by the way, used to carry horse-drawn stagecoaches across this same river but about thirty miles farther upstream.

The west buttress of the bridge is anchored in one of the canyon's first homesteads, the Mow claim. Whatever Mow lived in, it gave place to a stone cabin set against the far clay bank. Subsequent owners grew tired of the cabin's running water — wall to wall mud, actually — whenever a cloudburst hit the cliffs behind the house. They built the nucleus of the dwelling out on the knob above the river.

Still other owners enlarged the house from time to time and clustered it in ranchwork buildings. Now known as the Windy, from its exposed position to canyon drafts and the loquacity of a canyon resident, it is the winter headquarters of the Musser Cattle Company. From pioneer days the Musser family has absorbed one cattle outfit after another, until now its holdings cross or border the Escalante Road for most of its length, extend down the Gunnison between cliffs and river for many miles, and stretch back up the mountain in private pastures with concomitant public range use.

Though expanded and modernized (a microwave oven helps Bernice Musser with the old-fashioned job of cooking for crews of cowboys, and a calculator assists in the new-fangled job of preparing income tax returns) the Musser outfit still holds to some of the Old West practices that, for it, work best. While other cowmen hire semitrucks to haul cattle to range and market, the Mussers — third and fourth generation Jack and Tom and Johnnie — still move their cattle on the hoof. "We have good access to trails, and there's less risk of picking up foot disease."

Ever since the road started to bore under the plateau back there after the little swale-valley, the mountain has been helping the process by lifting the strata just a little faster than the slant of the eroding creek bed. This is why, in five miles or so from the river, the creek and road have cut down through the Dakota layers, through the reds, greens, purples, and grays of the Morrison (elsewhere bearer of dinosaur bone, uranium, bentonite, copper, amethyst, and other goodies), through the whites and pinks of Entrada, the red purple mudstones of Kayenta, the great cliff-forming, orange red Wingate sandstone, the ruby Chinle, right down to basement granite.

Scenically this is a hard act to compete with, but the stream manages, providing huge cottonwoods to shade bright-pebble waterfalls, green gold brookside meadows, thickets of willow, frothy tamarisk, and sweet summer clematis, as well as a fantastic variety of ditchbank marvels generally dubbed weeds.

The canyon is also special for its historic relics.

First buildings inside the canyon include the house that, according to popular belief, was built for a mail-order bride — in those days termed "heart and hand bride."

Old Bert Shreeves' descendents qualify the story a little:

"It's true, after his stepmother died he did need somebody to do the cooking, but he didn't just put a note in a box of apples going to Denver, the way you'd put a note in a bottle and cast it out to sea. When he put the note in the box it had a girl's name on it. He got the name from a friend."

However it came about, it worked out fine. Emma Roethenbach not only did the cooking, she took on the whole ranchwife routine.

This is as good a place as any to see how the ranchwife used her time in those days. Emma cooked for the family, for cowboys, and for hay crews that increased in number as the Shreeveses added lands and herds — serving food she herself largely produced from the garden patch, orchard, chicken house, hogpen, and milk barn. She churned butter, cured meat, canned and dried fruit, carried water in and slops out, and made bread, lye soap, quilts, and clothes for herself and the ten children she more or less incidentally gave birth to. The whole bit — wood cookstove, washboard, and backyard privy, plus stand-in duty as spare cowboy as needed.

All her children were born right on the ranch, with or without the help of a Delta doctor, depending on whether he could make the horseback ride in time.

Pioneering, it has been said, is hell on horses and women. Several Uncompahgre Plateau ranchers' wives couldn't stick it out. The phenomenal number (for those rigid times) of divorces and separations tells its own story.

But not Emma. For years on end she didn't even leave the canyon to go to the store in town. Every fall just before school started, the story goes, Old Bert lined his kids up, made cardboard patterns of their feet, and matched the patterns in store-bought shoes — about the only thing Emma couldn't make.

Maybe she was scared to go. The road into the canyon hasn't always been where it is now, nor half as easy. Farther up the canyon from the Shreeves place is the cliff-hung shelf that city-bred Emma had to come down to get into this hole. Maybe once down she was reluctant to trust her luck that far again.

Her son Bert explains, "You have to realize what that road was like. Took four horses to pull a buggy up it, six to a wagon. You never breathed till you'd passed a terrible narrow ledge-bend called the Elbow."

The place where Emma (and everybody else until 1926) came down can be seen from the ford where the Dry Fork Road branches left beside a peach orchard. It is the merest scar now, visible with binoculars high above the ford at the top of the cliff.

Down this route may have come the first wheels to touch the plateau. Before there was any kind of road into this slot, before the Indians went out, before the cattlemen and homesteaders came in, a bunch of freighters put their wagons down that bluff.

They were on their way between Utah and Pueblo. God knows how they came to be this far out of their way. Perhaps they had looked at some uncharted map, saw what looked like a shortcut, and underestimated the mountain the way pilots of light planes do now. Evidently they had beat winter this far but knew they'd never make it the rest of the way. Looking for a place with graze and shelter enough to get them and their oxen through the winter, they saw it down here, eased (probably logged) their wagons down, and afterward couldn't get them back up. Tearing one wagon apart, they roped their bedrolls and what grub was left onto one pair of wheels and hauled out, saving only their lives.

Nobody remembers anyone who saw the remains of the wagons or sign of the freight, but Brown Blumberg says when his dad and uncles came into the canyon the oxen left behind were still grazing canyon bottoms and benches.

Something called a road, a sidling shelf slightly cleared of boulders, was there when John Musser brought his family to his homestead in the upper end of the canyon in 1886. He didn't trust his children's safety to the wagon on that hill. One-year-old Don and little Edith, too small to walk down behind the wagon, were stuffed into panniers on either side of a packhorse — a mode of transportation so satisfactory that the two rode this way to summer camp every spring as long as they were small enough to squeeze into panniers.

The road wasn't a great deal better when Cap Smith made it up and down in his one-horse buggy. Everybody else drove wagons of one kind or another — spring or lumber — pulled by teams that walked in the ruts ground relatively smooth by the iron-shod wheels. Cap's mare had to cope with the middle, where any rocks that would pass under the axles were left undisturbed. It was a sporty rig, spindle-spoked, with a top that folded down in good weather and side curtains for rain. There was room in it for just two people or one person and a sack of flour.

"Plain useless," was the canyon consensus. "You couldn't haul enough groceries home to cook supper with — or chicken feed, or block salt. But Cap was sociable and was always tearing off to town in it."

Frank Ward remembers encountering Cap on that road.

Cap was a feisty little man who had left home (Joliet, Illinois) at the age of sixty-five. During the Civil War he had parlayed a month's duty as acting captain into a lifetime rank.

The road was too narrow for the two rigs to get around each other. Cap popped out of his buggy with all his feist frothing, "If you'd been whistling or singing or something, I'd of knowed you was coming and turned out at a wide place!"

Mentioning that he hadn't heard any whistling from Cap's direction either, Frank picked up the little buggy, hung it out on the rim of the road, squeezed his own team and wagon by, and set the buggy back in the tracks before going on.

The road was improved a little, but not much, for the

Model T Ford. Then in 1926 the entire route was changed to what is now a jeep road that trails back up the Dry Fork to easier climbing out of the canyon complex.

This road up the Dry Fork has had one unfortunate consequence. It passes near important Indian inscriptions that until the road came were known to few. Since then, and since the site had been placed on Forest Service maps, the Indian petroglyphs have been obliterated by the scrawls of vandals. They were important because they dated themselves; depicting chiefs riding horses, they could only have been made after the Indians acquired the horse following the Pueblo uprisings in 1680.

Chapter VII

TOMBSTONE CARVER'S CABIN

THAT ESCALANTE CANYON ever got a bridge across the Gunnison and a road out the lower end, instead of down the cliff face midway, is owing to the peach orchard beside the Dry Fork ford.

Oscar Huffington was a full-time cattleman with a summer camp on top of the mountain, spring-fall camp at Picket Corral, two, then three, wintering places along the Escalante, and another on Negro Gulch. He didn't need any more work or worries.

Ever since it was first settled, Escalante Canyon's cliff-enclosed sun pocket had been used to grow vegetables for freighting to the San Juan mining towns. Oscar said it would grow peaches.

People warned, "Maybe, but you can't truck peaches over that hill unless it's peach jam you expect to load onto the railroad cars."

They were almost right. By the time Oscar and his son Nelson had planted the second orchard, they and Old Bert Shreeves had started to work on the county commissioners. It took several years, Depression labor, and the gift of a bridge that a new highway had by-passed upstream at Austin. Road and bridge were put in by WPA (Works Progress Administration) labor and a minimum of money for gasoline from a county that in 1940 was very broke indeed.

If pioneering was hell for women, it wasn't exactly heaven for men. Oscar left some records of his workday and workyear that, except for the peaches, speak for all the other cattlemen.

There was the interminable riding. Cattle had to be

moved up to summer range, down to fall range, and farther
down to winter quarters, and wherever they were, checked
every few days.

Oscar rode up to close the poison fences in early spring,
to open them in early summer, to gather and brand calves,
separate weaners, put bulls and cows with small calves in
segregated pastures. He packed salt to the licks (about a ton
and a half of it, he once noted). He gathered market beef,
trailed them to the stockyards, and accompanied them on
their last ride to Denver sale yards. He spent days riding the
forest looking for strays. Though at one time he had five
hundred cows, and horses enough to handle them, like other
cattlemen he knew every critter by face and reputation. If
one was missing he searched till he found it.

"That bull I was out, found him up in the scrub oak,
brought him down to Cap's place. . . . Took the weaners
done to the pasture, cows with little calves up to Picket Corral. . . . Moved all my horses up to summer camp. . . . Rode
Old Cabin Bench and found 13 cows. . . . Brought 190 cows
down from Picket Corral, had to leave them at Alkali Beds,
too cold to ride."

Summer, spring, and fall, cows feed themselves, but in
winter they have to be fork fed. Every day Oscar or his hired
man climbed the frost-slick haystack, sliced off the day's ra-
tion with a hay saw, pitched the hay onto the wagon, and
forked it off on the frozen ground of the hayfield, relying on
the trained team to move the wagon at a rate that would
string out the hay, giving everybody — bossy and bossed —
an equal chance at breakfast. Since no one pasture could
hold them all, this operation went on at several places in
Oscar's winter holdings.

Between other jobs there was always something to be
built or rebuilt — fences, gates, corrals; hay stackers, hay
slings, hay skids; flumes, bridges, cellars, meat sheds, barns,
privies, a cistern. He had living quarters at four sites up and
down the mountain and was forever building or mending a
house, cabin, or bunkhouse, even painting the walls with
calcimine.

He had taken up raw land and never ceased expanding.

Every meadow, cornfield, and orchard cost him the labor of leveling gullies with horse-drawn plow and scraper, pulling trees, grubbing brush, and heaving rocks and boulders onto a stoneboat and dragging them away.

Then when he had conquered it, had the land working for him, it worked him — all the interminable irrigation, corn to plant, weed, and pick, hay to cut and stack, garden to plant, potato patch to dig.

These labors dovetailed between range-riding chores. He employed a hired man and occasional work crews. They had it easy, working only ten-hour days.

When there was nothing else to do — and even when there was — the eternally diminishing woodpile beside the kitchen door nagged to be replenished with logs snaked through the woods with horse and lariat, loaded on the wagon, hauled down, handsawed into stove length, and split. ·

Work dovetailed tighter after Oscar got into peaches. The peach year began slow and cold, with pruning and hauling the branches out of the orchard to riprap the stream against spring flood. It quickened with spraying and thinning, and climaxed to frenzy as the peaches colored — box nailer, labeler, picking and packing crews, crew cook, all to the lined up and synchronized with trucks and railroad cars — the last spasm between the moment the peach was too green to eat and too ripe to ship.

Men got hurt. They were thrown from horses; Oscar survived a broken rib that punctured his lung — and survived the trip to the hospital from off the mountain. They were thrown under wagon wheels; Henry Holland lost a leg that way. With little power equipment except their own muscles, they lifted too much; some died of strangulated hernia. There weren't enough men to do all the work, especially during World War II when men went to war or defense plants. Oscar wrote ruefully, "Worked the first female hay crew of my life."

Kids didn't have it easy, either. There is scarcely anything in these lists of male and female toil that children weren't expected to lend a hand with. Dillard says he was five years old when he was in the saddle helping his father separate weaner calves.

And the times had special deaths for children.

Diptheria struck the canyon following a dance. A teacher and one of her students sickened and died. Other children died at puzzling intervals of time and space. Though only two died at the Upper Canyon School, the frightened parents burned the schoolhouse to the ground, hoping to stop the epidemic.

Nelson Huffington, a boy at the time, describes those days:

"I was staying at Frank Wards, helping build fence. On a Sunday we were just riding around and came to the Bill Shreeveses about noontime. Door was open but nobody answered our holler, so we got down off our horses and went in. Table was all set, meat still warm, canned peaches, cream. Forks on the plates, a few bites gone. Beat us what could have yanked then away so complete and sudden, but we sat down and made a hearty meal.

"Then when folks found out we'd eaten where the diptheria victim ate, they wouldn't let us near. Mrs. Lockhart put out fumigant and medicine on a stump for us to take. I told Frank, 'I'm not going to take any of that stuff.' I didn't get it, but my Dad did. He gargled coal oil for a few days and got over it."

Along with responsibility, kids had a lot of independence, according to the memories of Frank Walker, who as a boy helped his father build the stone cabin just up the road from Huffingtons.

A bootlegger, loner named McElroy, lived up the canyon past the forks. I heard the revenuer say he was going up there to raid McElroy, and I got it into my kid head to ride up there and warn the old man. Rode so hard I had to change horses.

"After I told him, he asked me to see if I could find his liquor, and when I couldn't he showed me. Pulled out a set of shelves full of fruit jars, and there was four fifty-gallon barrels.

"Well, he gave me a big dinner of eggs and things and a

quart of the whiskey. I went down the road a ways, and I thought, well, why shouldn't I take a drink! Got down off my horse and had my drink and then couldn't get back on. It was a tall horse. Finally found a rock and got back up, but I didn't get home until about daylight."

The beautifully proportioned Walker stone cabin makes superb photographs from any angle but risky subject matter for painting — it is so perfect for its type it tends to look made-up on canvas.

When Harry Walker built it in 1911 he had a large family and little money. About the only thing the Walkers had going was Harry's skill as a bricklayer, his four sons' muscles, and plenty of raw material nearby. Unable to afford cement, they laid up the walls with mud mortar they dug from a hole in the yard, and mud is still all that holds the house together. The cement between the rocks is only skin deep, poked in later after they got money to buy it. Vandals have ripped out doors and windows, cattle horns have raked down the plaster, and their hooves have punched holes in the wood flooring. In spite of this, the house and fireplace still stand four-square and classic, a splendid advertisement for Harry's descendants, who are also bricklayers and stonemasons.

Visitors are as welcome as cows to roam the little house. It and the Walker homestead are state property, acquired by the Colorado Division of Wildlife.

Table Rock is a flat sandstone square (about ten feet square) capping the slender neck of a prong that is separated from the rest of the Wingate cliff by about three feet.

They tell that when Ben Lowe lived in the house under Table Rock it was his favorite stunt to jump his horse out onto the rock, make it rear, paw sky, and jump back across the gap. Scary trick, but not the one that killed him. He was also a crack shot, practiced at getting off a lightning-fast shot from under his horse's neck.

On the day of his death Ben Lowe was riding down the canyon with his two small sons when he was overtaken by lawman Cash Sampson. For some time the two men had had a feud going, egged on by "friends" on both sides. Anticipating a fight, Lowe sent his children on ahead. From over the next hill the boys heard loud quarreling and then shooting. They raced back to find Sampson dead, their father dying.

With no survivors or witnesses to the shoot-out it was never known what the specific quarrel was about or who drew gun first. The one bullet missing from Cash's gun entered Ben's body low in the back, emerging from the upper chest — a trajectory only probable if he had been bent over his horse, shooting from under the neck.

Since Ben Lowe had been involved in the Sheep War a few months earlier, and Sampson was investigating it, most people assumed the duel stemmed from that. There were some rumors that Lowe had been rustling horses and taking them over the mountain to sell to the Indians, but a flamboyant man like Lowe spawned rumors. There were also rumors that it was Ben's horse that left hoof marks in the wooden floor of the John Davis clothing store on one of his "shooting up Main" Saturday nights in town. John says this is definitely not true, it was Shorty Gibson who left those tracks — still there. Ben rode his horse into the saloon next door that night.

Escalante Canyon is most widely known as the site of Cap Smith's cabin.

Capt. Henry A. Smith was a tombstone carver by trade. When he came west in his old age and took up land in the canyon he laid up three rock walls against a great slab of sandstone standing on edge at the foot of a high red cliff. On the outside of the slab wall he carved his name and rank in big letters. On the inside he carved a bed-sized alcove in which he slept — some say on the bare rock shelf with a piece of stovewood for pillow — and which he intended to be his crypt after death. Fate tricked him out of the latter; he died while on a visit to California and was buried under grass. Beside the bed niche he carved another, tall and slender, where he kept his guns.

High on the cliff above the house he carved his initials and the name of an old crony who used to come out from Delta to play cards with him, R. Bowen, a blacksmith.

History hides in thickets. These wheels carried the bodies of Ben Lowe and Cash Sampson off the plateau after their shoot-out.

Under Bowen's name Cap carved the horseshoe enclosing a star that was the standard insignia of the blacksmith shop.

Cap was a sociable man. A one-bed cabin was far too small.

For one thing, his place was about midway of the two ends of the canyon and about midway between the top of the mountain and town. People on the short trip stopped for noon dinner; people on the long haul tended to stay overnight. His diary reads like a guest book in Grand Central Station. The days when nobody at all stopped in were so rare they got special notation. If he wasn't having company he was incurring social debts by *being* company — off to town to canyon parties and schoolhouse dances. To stay even he built another rock house with beds below and in the loft. The back wall of this cabin is equipped with a set of hinged shelves like McElroy's, but Cap's is supposed to have concealed the secret place where he kept his meat supply — out-of-season venison that in his diary was always referred to in code as "fresh air." "Otto [his son] went out for some fresh air but didn't find any."

Cap lived on the gold coins of his Civil War pension, on what he grew in his two small fields and garden, and by carving tombstones for less durable neighbors.

At one time cemeteries all over the western part of the state had examples of his work — roses, twining ivy, oak-leaf sprays, sentimental verses beautifully carved in tawny or rosy sandstone. But sandstone weathers easily and proved to be no match for the automatic sprinkling systems that came, fortunately for his pride, after his death.

By the time the canyon has bored into the mountain as far as Cap's place it has reached basement rock. Cap took advantage of the stream's narrow slot through granite to put his dam where the water fell from the lifted lip of hard rock down to soft sandstone. The dam the old man built of rocks, poles, brush, and dirt is still there, though often replaced by him and subsequent owners after spring floods.

Like Walker cabin and Picket Corral, Cap's place is now state owned, acquired by the Colorado Division of Wildlife to provide winter browse for deer and habitat for small

Cap Smith's red rock slab cabin in Escalante Canyon. The black granite inner canyon begins beyond the cottonwoods.

game. In recognition that Cap's place is probably the most visited spot on the mountain, the division has also provided human feeding facilities — a picnic table and fireplace.

Although Escalante was in early days the most populated part of the Uncompahgre, the miles between Cap's place and The Forks are almost untouched by the hand of man.

The creek is out of reach of the irrigation shovel, chuckling along in its deep, black canyon under narrow, sage-silvered benches banded with glittering quartz and schists so ancient they look like crumbling coal banks. Overhead, orange red cliffs push and pull, opening doors to further views, rising from great mounds of boulder-studded, garnet red Chinle that here, as in Unaweep, provides soft roadbed riding on granite.

Over everything, growing on anything that isn't purely perpendicular, are the black green desert trees, juniper and pinyon, spaced out according to the moisture room each root system mines, even and random like ink spatterings covering a vast abstract painting.

The most magnificent feature of this section of the canyon is the great drapery of talus slopes sweeping down from somewhere high out of sight, glacial grandeur of frozen motion flowing down over the tall red cliffs, burying them, flowing on. Gray white, they are the ghostly remnant of white cliffs, long eroded over the rim of the world, cliffs whose size can only be guessed from the mass of material they left in retreating.

In deep bays between the talus tongues, water has eroded the white deposit, exposing the Wingate cliff and shadowy, undercut caves below. The water that created the coves has peopled them with pinnacles — white columns under protective rock caps tilted at the rakish angle of the talus from which they were carved.

For miles the twisting red road passes these bays like stage sets, one after another — white ruins of skyscrapers silhouetted against a shadowy cave, spectators in a stadium, cliff dwellings so real you must climb and touch to disprove cliff dwellers themselves, lined up to watch your alien car pass by.

Golden cottonwood leaves float through reflections in Escalante Creek.

The Forks is the end of the Escalante Road. Everything beyond requires pickup or four-wheel drive — at least for peace of mind.

When John Musser homesteaded he built his headquarters here where the branches of the Escalante converge, giving his cattle easy access to the mountain or directly onto one of the intervening "points," where they were at once on summer range.

At the Forks he built two connected log cabins. They were still the ranch home when his youngest son, Kel, got married.

In view of the hard labor expected of a ranchwife it obviously behooved a cattleman to pick a husky woman, but Kel Musser married a tiny girl, the product of a young ladies' academy back East who had been taught to play the organ and mandolin, speak French, and elocute in English. Eda was an expert horsewoman on the English saddle and expert at driving a varnished phaeton behind spirited ponies. She refused to ride a western stock saddle. "Too uncomfortable." The ranch horses refused to wear her little pancake saddle. "Too undignified," their actions implied as they kicked it off — and to pieces, if possible. She couldn't cook, either.

Kel built her a big house and taught her how to cook.

"I'm still a cowboy cook, she says. "Meat, potatoes, and pie. Lots of it and on short notice."

But she was tough (she could swing herself across the river on a basket cable) and she wasn't timid. When the sheriff, posse, and several of the curious headquartered at the Forks while a canyon death was being investigated, she laid down the law to the law.

"The sheriff and the others had a lot of guns, and I told him when they came in to eat and spend the night, 'You just put your guns away somewhere. I've small children here, and all this crowd and feelings so high, something bad might happen.' So he did."

As times changed for Eda and other ranchwives, the chores became less those of producing and preparing food and other commodities, and more of handling the outfit's

Cattle and corrals at The Forks. Dust at left is raised by cattle cutting in the corrals. Old, hand-powered gasoline pump supplies Musser family vehicles.

paperwork — banking, bookkeeping, government reports, breeding records, and income tax returns.

"It was natural that ranchwomen should take over the finances," Eda explains. "They lived in town all winter, putting the children in school. Bankers were more used to the wives' faces and signatures than those of the men — who usually are too busy on the range to come to town when a loan or a new truck is needed."

From the Forks the Escalante begins its tree-branch structure. Jeep roads branch from here but in some cases encounter padlocked gates where private property must be crossed to reach public lands.

One branch goes to Picket Corral, another to the Calhoun winter camp, and beyond it the Crabill summer camp where gold and not stray cows was the pursuit. Frank Ward and Mrs. Fred Crabill tell about it:

"Family just kept pecking away. Every time they'd give up, somebody would find another little pocket of gold and they'd get all enthused again. There just had to be a vein somewhere.

"One summer Ma Crabill found a chunk of rock out on the dump, so heavy she sent it off to the Denver assay. That kept them fired up for a while. But there was no way to tell which one of the pockholes it had come from.

"They'd have quit years before they did, but — lucky or unlucky — there was money in the family on one side or the other. Banking and the Delta Flour Mill."

The North, or Spring, Fork of the Escalante brings most of the perennial water to the stream and was a favorite winter home for Indians at Sawtell (named for its last, not its first, resident). Their village extended clear across the canyon bottom. About fifty years ago the earth in and around the circular walls of the village was excavated by the Colorado Museum of Natural History, which determined that the site had had long and continuous occupancy and as late as three hundred years ago. Only that part of the village lying on the far side of the creek, a little harder to get at, survived the homesteaders.

To understand what happened, and not to be too cen-

Indian ruins lie across the North Fork of the Escalante. Morgan Henderson worked cattle on the Uncompahgre all his adult life.

sorious from our different viewpoint in time, we should be a little more understanding of other ways and other times than the homesteaders were when they "vandalized" the part of the Indian village on their side of the creek.

Early settlers (in pure, sincere, and innocent conviction) believed they were supplanting a vacuum of culture with something vastly superior. They believed the Indian himself would either recognize this and accept it or would justifiably suffer from "stubborn and lazy" failure to do so. Only far distant from the brunt of pioneering did the sentiment of the noble savage find expression in that century.

One of those pioneers, Ray Burritt, wrote concerning the removal of the Utes from their Uncompahgre Reservation.

He noted the Indians' "present and long-continued occupancy of much-desired range lands and thousands of acres of lands which could be cleared for agriculture," and he continued, "The Indians would not, nor could not, make any use of these idle ranges or farm lands.

"That being so," he asked, "then why should our own people be denied that God-given opportunity to create new homesites for the thousands of land-hungry citizens from those Reservation lands?"

Thus with no trace of compunction the first homesteader pried out and carried off all those nice flat rocks to wall his potato cellar, probably thanking God at morning prayers for putting them there so handy.

His own culture, the pioneer culture, now is archeological artifact — the cookstove left when his house burned after many years, some weathered boards that were his barns. . . .

Chapter VIII

DINOSAUR DIG

MONUMENT HILL is one of three bumps on the "lofty mountain lying down" considered worthy of naming.

The name does not indicate any imposing Christ-of-the-Andes statuary erected on the crest, though something like that might have been timely when the feud between the two ends of Montrose County heated up, as we shall see farther up the road. Monument Hill is a survey point, the first, establishing all others on the plateau — that is, first after the wildcat one that slightly missed the mark in Escalante Canyon.

As mountains go, the Uncompahgre isn't all that high, only two miles. Its uniqueness is in maintaining so much of it at that level. It is this lofty level that makes the plateau crest as susceptible to lightning bolts as higher and more pointed peaks are known to be.

The mountain demonstrates this not far from Monument. The Divide Road here is running just under the slope of the crest. On the skyline to the left two dark globs in the tops of two dead aspens look like microwave discs. When you climb up there, through thigh-deep sage, wild roses, and lupine, you come out into a circle of death. The growth stops short as if cut back with shears. All the aspens, white as chalk strokes, claw leafless at the sky, except for those two weird globular branches. It happened a while ago; weather has washed the ashes of the fire away, and roses and sage are coming back, inch-high between the pale, flat rocks. The circle is fascinating and frightening, like a fairy circle in the lawn. Realizing what caused it, you scan the sky. If it is dark you hurry back to the car, not waiting for the ends of your hair to tingle and lift in the mountaintop warning that inscrutable negatives are flowing underfoot, seeking just that tiny elevation — perhaps your head — that would channel them to arc explosion in the sky.

Just beyond Monument Hill signs point in opposite directions to the Club Cow Camp on the west and Calhoun Cow Camp on the east. J. D. Dillard describes the setting of the old Club:

"It lay right under the Tongue where they ran their horses. Reason it was called the Tongue, from up on the divide it looks like a big tongue stuck out at the valley, pointed off toward Calamity and Outlaw."

At one time Club and Calhoun range was all one. The Club outfit went straight over the plateau and down the other side like an enormous Spanish saddle blanket, the fringes dragging river bottoms on either side. The town of Uravan sits on part of it, the town of Delta just misses.

Club's final eastern extension was made after Dillard turned twenty-one, old enough to take up a claim on his own. The cabin at the Whickie, as his place was called, was built to give Club cowboys someplace to stay while wintering cows on that side of the range. In keeping with early-day energy-saving devices, the log cabin walls were built double, the intervening space stuffed with sawdust for insulation. The sawdust and the logs themselves, if ever such a cabin caught fire, could produce a smelter-hot blaze. If you come onto the ashes of a log cabin it is nothing to find solidified glass dribbles that were bottles. You may even find solidified iron dribbles that were once the stove.

Dillard's 640-acre homestead included Fat Man's Misery, a slot in a stretch of cliff along the Roubideau that only skinny people can squeeze through. In the days of horse and buggy, Fat Man's Misery was just the right distance from Delta for Sunday picnics and Saturday night hayrides — then, as times changed, for beer busts and pot parties.

A large open area east of the Club-Calhoun saddle was known by old-timers as Indian Park. Dillard explains:

"For a lot of years after the Utes were moved onto their

Utah desert reservation they came back to their Uncompahgre hunting grounds in big bands, taking upwards of a thousand deer. Those that ranged out in the country around this part of the Divide would pack the deer into this park, bringing the heads, too, because they used the brains to tan the hides.

"They'd be there a long time. Old cowboy Charley Collins says he counted seventy-five empty deer heads in this park after they left.

"My mother said one year the Indians were awful thick around here, and there was a big smoke over on the La Sal Mountains. Whatever that smoke meant, the next day the Indians were all packed up and leavin'. They trailed off the mountain for a whole day, and they never did come back in big numbers again. Just a few at a time."

Your fourth saddle view after Monument Hill will be the last for a while. Bear Pen Gulch takes off to the left from here, and Dillard has the story of how it got its name:

"Happened when I was seven or eight years old. Some varmint had caught a mare of Oscar Huffington's up on the hillside above Love Mesa there. They came down off, a-tearin' up quakies as big as your arm, and he killed her right at the foot of the hill.

"Dad came along the same day and went back home for a bear trap which he set — inside a pen, of course, so the cattle couldn't get at it.

"Well, there was a Duval executive from New York stayin' with us, out here for his health, and he was greatly interested in this bear trap. He wanted to get a foot or tooth or something off the bear if they caught him. This was awful big bear country at that time. Lot of old silvertips.

"Couple days later, when Dad went to look at the trap, Langdon went along. There was a mountain lion in it, and Langdon said, 'Don't shoot him, Jeff. Let me get a club and kill him. That'll be someting to tell when I get back to New York — killed a mountain lion with a club!'

"Old lion just layin' there, eatin on the horse, whippin' back and forth. He'd slapped his tail in the trap, and tail's all was holding him, and it about off.

"Langdon walked up, and that lion jumped and made a pass at him, and he came runnin' out of there backwards, hollerin' 'Shoot him, Jeff! Shoot him!'

"So they reset the trap. When they came back three days later they'd caught a big old silvertip. He took that trap and a big old heavy green quakie log way up the canyon before he gave up and died. Bear don't live too long in a trap.

"Langdon cut one of his feet off. I remember that foot, I've never seen a foot like that. My golly, that was a tremendous thing!

"He laid it on a stone out there by the saddle shed while we ate dinner, intendin' to skin it out and have it mounted. Well, do you know, he never got that foot to New York, either. Our old dog Junior buried it, and Langdon never could find where."

The Love Mesa sign along the roadside indicates not a romantic activity but the homeplace of an early cowman, John Love. Love's cabin may have been the last of the original settlers' dwellings to go, being fitted together entirely with wooden pegs, no nails. Part of its chimney still stands. In fact, the cabin outstayed its builder — Love was one of the early plateau dropouts.

At this point you are about as close as you can get on this road to the Dry Mesa dinosaur dig.

Though the dig is about halfway between you and the Delta sugar silos, it would be about as easy to take a time warp into the dinosaur age as to get to that rim from where your wheels are standing. To drive there you would have to go all the way down to Delta and back up another road. That thirty-five-mile logging road crosses some rough country, barely traversable by car but clearly marked.

The dig is open only during those summers when Dr. James Jensen of Brigham Young University (Dinosaur Jim to the paleontological world) can raise the several thousand dollars it takes for two months of crew and equipment. At other times the bone quarry is carefully bulldozed over with earth to protect the remaining rare skeletons from weather and vandals.

Dinosaur dig on the rim of Dry Mesa, looking down the East Fork of Escalante Canyon. The "world's largest bone," an eight-foot shoulder blade, is in the foreground.

The Dry Mesa dinosaur bone deposit was the third and largest prehistoric discovery made on the plateau by Vivian and Eddie Jones of Delta. The first was in Potter Basin, a seven-foot femur that, as "the world's largest bone," is now on display in the Smithsonian Institution. The second was in the Dominguez area, the forty-foot skeleton of a lizardlike animal previously unknown to science.

This bonepile on Dry Mesa seems to be an almost inexhaustible rick of bones swept together like driftwood in floodwaters some 150 million years ago. The find includes several species never before known. One of them is a flying lizard-serpent. Another is, once again, "the largest bone in the world," an eight-foot shoulder blade of a creature that stood 60 feet high when he walked the earth.

The Joneses, who are amateur paleontologists with a firm respect for expertise, called on professional help in uncovering each find. Dr. Jensen says that since the bones in this prticular dig are earthy rather than stony in texture they are very fragile and will not bear their own weight if mounted. He has promised that the university will provide a full-length, full-strength replica of the skeleton for local display — whenever a six-story building is erected to house it.

T-Bone Springs Campground on the Divide Road just past Bear Pen Gulch was named during the Great Depression by the men who were building the Divide Road as we know it now.

Before that the road along the plateau crest was a rather spotty and sometime thing — fair in stretches where loggers and miners had smoothed off wagon access to certain stands of timber or outcrops of ore, but just about nonexistent between those stretches.

To provide income for men out of work during the depression, and at the same time to get something needed in return for the public money expended, the government built the Divide Road and its campgrounds with WPA and CCC (Civilian Conservation Corps) funds and labor. The former were mainly local family men, and the latter were mainly teenagers from Eastern cities.

Dr. James Jensen "Dinosaur Jim" stretches out alongside the 150-million-year-old shoulder blade. He and his crew from Brigham Young University work the Dry Mesa dig every summer that weather and financing permit.

Eddie and Vivian Jones hunt dinosaur bone with a Geiger counter. In pursuit of her activities as rockhound, and his as lumber-mill owner, their four feet have probably stepped on more square inches of Uncompahgre Plateau than those of any other two people now alive.

Aspens are capable of anything. Saner trees, having the top nipped out, hold a committee meeting and appoint one branch to carry on as a main trunk. This tree, near T-Bone Spring, apparently came to a schizophrenic compromise.

They received $30 per month plus board and bed. The CCC boys were also provided with work clothes, shapeless blue denim fatigues in one size only — too big. The boys were encouraged, but not required, to send most of their pay back home to the folks, and some actually did. Some, who became interested in local girls and local dances, used part of their pay to hire town women to cut their baggy fatigues to a more flattering fit.

At that time hamburger was spoiling in the stores at twelve cents a pound because people didn't have the twelve cents. Cattlemen were no better off. Not only were they unable to sell their steers because nobody had any money, but the depression coincided with one of the worst droughts in this century. There was no hope of simply holding the cattle on grass until times got better; they were starving on the range.

The government came to their rescue, too, buying up the skinny cows for nominal sums. The worst of them were shot and buried in trenches with teams and scrapers. The better ones were butchered (also with WPA labor) and the meat given to the crews and to families on relief (almost everybody), both locally and in cities elsewhere.

Men working in the Divide Road camps, who had been eking out on bread and beans, suddenly were living high on the cow, and they named this work camp accordingly. They made a vow never to eat anything but T-bone steak at this place, and, indeed, the "Class of 1930-39" did actually hold reunions here on several occasions, celebrating the time and place with a big steak feed.

The building of the Divide Road marks a watershed in road construction between horse-man power and heavy equipment. It was perhaps a little late in coming to the plateau; pioneering here extended longer into the twentieth century than in other areas.

Morgan Hendrickson describes the impact when the power source moved from the front of the scraper, pulling, to behind it, pushing:

"After the Divide Road got toward the south end, they

Evergreens and aspens border mountaintop slickrock glade like boys and girls around a dance floor.

came in here with a Caterpillar tracter dozer, first we ever saw.

"Bert Carver was road boss. He had crews out ahead of the teams working with pick and shovel to make some kind of shelf or ditch along the steep hillsides to give footing for the horses that pulled the plows and scrapers. Naturally he did the same thing getting ready for the Caterpillar, looping a ditch up around a log draw. Took three weeks to make that loop-ditch with picks and shovels; the Cat took one day to make a road for itself straight across the draw. Bert was so flabbergasted he was mad. All but jumped up and down on his hat."

As you probably noticed shortly before T-Bone Springs, the shape of the crest has clenched up. No open, expansive saddle glades along here. The road narrows, hugging in under a series of rocky knobs, and there is a whole lot of nothing below your starboard hub caps. Trees along the skyline (that's directly overhead) are flying their branches all on one side, like flags frozen in a gale.

The edge of the narrowing road isn't the only thing you have to watch along here. For some reason this stretch of road is a favorite hangout for idle cows. Probably they are tired of standing on a slant down in that vertical scenery, and there is certainly no place else level enough to lie down.

In rounding any curve be prepared to come to a complete stop and wait while the cows study the make and model of your car and decide whether you are worth moving over for. They know damn well the entire state of Colorado belongs to them — and it does, at at least the legal right-of-way does, especially up here. Remember, back at Mudhole picnic grounds it was the campers not the cows that were fenced in.

While the cows are making up their minds, take a look over that vast cavity on your right. Part of it was chewed out by a creek named for an animal even stubborner than the ones blocking your car.

Burro Creek is the place the little "four-legged miners" emigrated when they were turned loose to scrounge for

Horse-drawn grader of the vintage that constructed the Divide Road has never left the plateau.

themselves at the time the local mines went broke between World Wars I and II.

Nobody went into an ecological tizzy about the plight of the abandoned species. The whole world knows that the burro can cope. These not only coped, they multiplied, for many years furnishing a source of transportation for Nucla kids, whose favorite sport was roping and breaking the miniature broncs.

Burros named the creek, and the creek named a whole layer of this earth's surface, wherever else it occurs.

Geologists have a practice of calling a stratum of rock by the name of the place where it first and best comes to their attention. The layer of rock that immediately underlies the Dakota sandstone cap of the plateau, way up here, was first brought to their attention on Burro Creek, way down there in that tangle of canyons opening off the San Miguel.

What's it doing down there? We'll find out at Windy Point a little farther on.

Chapter IX

WINDY POINT ROCK BOOK

AT WINDY POINT the vertebral chain of knobs you have been driving under for a mile or so continues in the same general direction, southwest, culminating in Spruce Mountain. The 47 Cow Camp Trail follows this spine to the camp down on the far slopes of Spruce, but the road and the divide do not.

The North Fork of Tabeguache Creek here cuts back into the plateau in a beautiful curve behind the Spruce Mountain ridge, creating a jog in the precise but often imperceptible line that separates east and west streams. The knobby spine is only a spur of the mountain proper, like vestigial tailbones.

From Windy Point the real divide cuts sharply to the left, eases down a gentle slope, and turns again southwest to resume the normal saddle pattern a little beyond Porter Cow Camp. But the saddles are becoming less and less apparent as the mountain gradually climbs and forests thicken.

Don't leave Windy Point quite yet. If you don't stop anywhere else on the Divide Road, you should stop at Windy Point. Here is where the scenery best explains what this mountain has been up to for the past 600 million years.

The part of it that falls away at your feet below this spectacular point really fell — about four thousand feet, measuring by where the Burro Creek layer landed.

Or perhaps it only seems to have fallen. Actually, the plateau cracked along the full length of its western edge, lifted, and tilted back like a box lid partially opening. This is what makes the abrupt west face of the mountain so indifferent from the slanting east side.

The Uncompahgre Uplift, responding to tides within the molten globe, has done its rising-sinking act a number of times in those millions of years, but always with a movement so undetectably slow that, for all we can tell, it may be going on under our feet as we stand here — motion no more perceptible to us (or from century to century) than the tidal lift and fall of a ship moored to a pier is from second to second to a man standing at shiprail above the dock.

At Windy Point you are viewing some very peculiar landscape. This hundred-mile-long fault is repeated in parallel faults, rank on rank, as far west as you can see. Paradox Valley lies between the first pair; a long strip sank between two faults as the Uncompahgre rose. Salt Valley in Arches National Monument and Lisbon Valley near Moab were simularly created.

During the eons when the uplift bore all the 350 million years' worth of accumulated earth-stuff we noted as "missing pages" back at the granite quarry on Unaweep, the eroding mountain heights shucked off strata in stupendous quantities, piling onto the fault troughs and pushing them ever farther down by sheer weight of rock.

Something had to give, and salt deposits can give. Under pressure, natural rock salt can flow like glacial ice (which is perhaps why the government reconsidered stashing radioactive waste in "eternally safe" Kansas salt mines).

Deep in the earth, beneath almost everything you can see out there, is an immensely wide salt bed four thousand feet thick. As the debris from the Uncompahgre Uplift piled deeper and heavier the salt squeezed up through the long slots of the faults "like toothpaste," as geologist Donald L. Baars describes it, "sixteen thousand feet deep."

The extruding salt would have formed long ridges, except that salt formations leach away faster than other kinds of rock when exposed to weathering, so instead of hogbacks the salt outcrops formed valleys. The Dolores River, cutting across Paradox Valley, taps one of these salt deposits and contaminates Colorado River water for everybody downstream. Sinbad Basin on the slopes of the La Sals (Sal *means* salt!) is an oval hole in the ground created by long-departed salt that found its way into the San Miguel River through a crack in the basin rim called Salt Creek Canyon.

It is proposed to sink wells and pump the salt-laden groundwater away from the Dolores, but the project has something of the feel of trying to sweeten San Francisco Bay by spooning out the Pacific Ocean. Sixteen thousand feet! And perhaps still squeezing, squeezing up.

And when the salt water has been pumped to the surface, what do we do with it? Dried in settling ponds, it will blow in the wind; wet, it will eventually get into the drinking water sometime, somewhere. Nothing, but nothing, stays put on this planet, where even the pieces of the earth's crust bob up and down to their own time scale like chips on a pond.

After so much grubbing around below ground trying to figure out what's going on down there, it is a relief to look up and simply take in the Windy Point view for what it offers now, this last quarter of the twentieth century. Immensity. Blue ridge on blue ridge, paling into distance, punctuated by the darker violet of the La Sal and Abajo mountains. Beyond them, a faintly warmer line on the far horizon, is the red plateau of Utah and Canyon Lands.

Even out there we don't get away from the plateau's past. Some of the Uncompahgre Uplift material laid down the formations from which Canyon Lands sculpture was carved.

In eons of desert between eons of prehistoric seas, winds scoured red rock into red sand, drifted it west where it became rock again. Now in fantastic sculpture it is weathering once more to sand and silt, still moving on the wind and down the Colorado to recycle into new red landscapes. Deposits being laid down now in the Gulf of California, and in the dammed lakes between, may rise to reveal new pages made of the same old book.

Some idea of the enormity of time and material that have come and gone in this place can be gained by imagining how much solid rock would have to be piled on top of those La Sals to suppress a volcano, because that is what happened. When lava tried to surface there, the strata above it were so deep the molten rock could only squeeze between layers in a lens-shaped bulge called a lacolith. It hardened, the covering strata wore completely away, and now even the dense rock of the lava dome has eroded into peaks and canyons.

The view at Windy Point is enjoyed by permanent residents, a pair of eagles. You may be lucky enough to see one hanging out there, motionless in the air, supported by the great, invisible roller wind-wave mentioned earlier. If, like small airplanes, he has problems with the downdraft on the lee side, he can probably overfly the turbulence, being engineered with better aerodynamics, and having the kind of fuel injection system that doesn't ice up.

As the forest thickens it is more and more rare to find views off both sides of the mountain at once. Where they do occur in the stretch between Porter Cow Camp and Smokehouse Campground, the mountain best reveals its basic shape — a vast schoolyard slide. The long ramp to the east from the crest "landing" is reached on the west by a steep ladder of broken strata.

If you leave your car and go exploring for such a view (or for any reason) you needn't worry about getting lost, no matter how far you go, if you remember that on this contrary mountain the advice is just the opposite to the usual "follow the stream downhill and you will eventually come to civilization." "Eventually" here could be a stroll of twenty to seventy miles. Instead, follow the drainage — stream or ravine — *uphill* and you cannot fail to come out on the Divide Road, though if you make a lateral miscalculation your car may turn up "missing" and you'll have to walk on up or back down the road to the place where you parked it.

Not far from Windy Point is Jeff Lick, named for Jeff Dillard, about the last of the old salt "stomps" to retain name and identity — at least on the map. Jeff Lick also stands for a Dillard cattle brand, JEF, which Oscar Huffington bought along with JEF range when he was putting together his two-phase outfit down on the Escalante.

Stock salt was first transported by packmule then by

wagon — where a wagon could negotiate the terrain. J. D. Dillard recalls:

"U-C, Mussers, and the Club always hired salt haulers. Took an expect skinner and four good horses to put a wagon over some of those cliff-hung trails without rollin'. If you had much of a load you'd better have six head.

"I was foolish enough to make one trip with the old boy who for years did the salt hauling.

"Before daylight he'd put his coffee on the campfire, harness up, hang the morrells on the horses' heads, and stand there watchin' 'em eat oats while drinkin' his coffee — all the breakfast he took time for. The minute the last horse quit eatin', that old boy jerked the morrells off, put the bridles on, hooked up, and was on his way. And me a growin' boy needin' sleep and grub!

"He was quite a man," Dillard's voice dwindles off, "and I can't even remember his name."

But J. D. was leaning about salt hauling, one of a myriad of things he would need to know when later he began to work his father's outfit, and still more when he assumed duties with the Forest Service and as a salaried representative of the cattlemen's association.

Boys expected to learn directly from men how to live as men. Girls learned their lifework from women. All ages worked together. A relatively small fraction of youth was spent segregated in school-environment peer groups, resulting in a homogenous society with an unforced, unstudied empathy with those of different age.

Another of Dillard's early memories is an instance:

"This Easterner Langdon sold his relinquishment down on the Roubideau to Ash Price. Price got awfully ill with rheumatism. Poor old fellow. We, his son and I, used to catch him bees in the holly oak. He'd heard that was good, and he'd put them on his legs and let them sting him. But he didn't live too many years."

Neither wagons nor jeeps completely outmoded the packhorse for distributing salt; the licks must be widely scattered to spread the grazing into areas accessible only by trail.

It took a lot of salt, partly because the cattlemen were willy-nilly supplying seasoning for the summer diet of wild game that couldn't be expected to tell the difference between government and private salt. On one occasion Oscar Huffington notes how much and for whom: "Packed out 3,500 pounds of rock salt. . . . The deer ought to do fine, as well as the cows."

A mile or so beyond where the 47 Pack Trail crosses the road from one side of the mountain to the other, an unnamed spring and a jog in the road mark the approximate vicinity of Nasty Park, also mentioned earlier. You'll have to find it for yourself, off in the woods to the left somewhere, because no sign on road or map identifies it. Obviously the Forest Service would like to forget the whole thing. Clues: The park is said to be round in shape and not far from Twin Lakes — but since there are two possible sets of twin lakes, that's not much help. If you inquire directions of any cattleperson, gentleman or lady, you'll have to use the original four-letter version, or they won't know what you're talking about.

The abundant wildlife on the plateau does not include a noticeable number of rattlesnakes, but at this spring you are in a direct downhill line (but luckily more than two steep miles) from a bench that is so thickly populated by these varmints it goes by the name of Rattlesnake.

Dillard describes place and problem:

"Rattlesnake is the next bench above the Indian racetrack behind Little Round Mountain. Snakes were so thick there that stockmen resorted to dynamite to eradicate 'em. There's one den of the damned things in there that nobody ever did blast out. Fortunately the snakes stayed put on that bench and never did come on up to the top of the hill."

Rattlesnake Bench is also in the general vicinity of the place where people say the McCarty Gang cached that gold, which may be part of the reason nobody has found it.

Catching its highest snowmelt in the neighborhood of this same spring on the Divide Road is the Dry Fork of Escalante Creek — and snowmelt is about all the water it gets, just the early summer runoff.

In Denver and on east, people who could raise a little cash had no way of knowing how dry Dry Fork really was when speculators hit them with the chance to get in on the ground floor of an irrigation project that would make a watered Eden of thousands of acres of desert on the lower slopes of the mountain. The full length of Sawmill Mesa and all its benches from treeline right down to the Roubideau were to be irrigated by the Dry Fork Project. According to Morgan Hendrickson, "It would take all the water in the Gunnison Tunnel to irrigate that much land."

Money flowed in. A four hundred foot trestle flume was constructed, and about nine miles of impressive ditch were scooped out along the shoulders of Grade Gulch. Money was all that flowed. Not a drop of water coursed the canal, which was even engineered dry, as another old-timer explains: "Beautiful ditch. Only thing was, it ran the wrong way."

The story behind Smokehouse Springs Campground is as hard to pin down as a whiff of the smoke that names it.

Anyone who has ever listened to sincere eyewitnesses giving varying details about an incident that happened last week will not be surprised that events of more than seventy five years ago can be remembered differently by different participants, especially if the memories are not those of participants at all but second hand from father or grandfather. But there is considerable agreement that:

"The Utes built the smokehouse and used it to 'make meat' every year in hunting season. That's where they made deer jerky for their winter meat supply. The smoke wasn't to cure the meat, the way we cure pork, but just to keep the flies from laying maggot eggs in it."

Apparently it was when a good share of the deer jerky turned out to be made of cattlemen's beef that the summit meeting was called at Nasty Park.

Jerky is simply dried meat. Smoke may improve the flavor and shorten the drying, but isn't vital. You may make jerky by cutting red meat in thin strips and hanging them over a clothesline to dry in open air and sun. In that case, to keep the flies off you dust the meat liberally with black pepper first — also improves the flavor. It's about the consistency of sole leather when done, whatever cut it comes from, and consequently can be made from even the toughest part of the critter.

You eat jerky raw, out of hand, biting off chews of it like plug tobacco, or you pound it into a powdery pulp (traditionally with a hammer on the butt end of a cedar log) and make gravy of it. Delicious.

The naming of Smokehouse Springs is differently told in Forest Service records. They state it was built by one of the racehorse Roberts brothers, also for making jerky. But whether they jerked deer, their own cows, or somebody else's cows, the record does not say.

Chances are both accounts are right; the Roberts brothers saw the Indians had a good thing going and replaced their pole smokehouse (which was probably no more than an enlarged sweathouse in shape) with a building made of lumber. Nothing remains of either structure.

At Smokehouse Springs if you walk over the little rise to your right and down to the rim you will be almost directly above another of the mountain's paradoxes — a mine too rich to work.

In referring to the problems at the Copper King, Carl Smith cites those of a more famous ore outcrop to the west, the Cashin Copper Mine.

"Just veins of pure copper, too pure and soft to mine. You couldn't drill it with a single jack; the drill just wedged in tight. Couldn't blast it; dynamite just made a pothole, pushing the copper around like gummy mush.

"It's had a lot of owners, each one looking at that pure metal and figuring he'd be the one smart enough to find a way to get it out of the ground. But anything anybody ever tried always cost more money and work than they got out of it.

"If they tried to mine around it, bringing out matrix and all, the metal just gummed up the ball mill.

"One fellow thought he'd dissolve it with acid, catch the solution, and refine the copper out of it. Brought in two barrels of acid on muleback and poured it in the vein. It just kept right on going — clear to China, I guess."

Chapter X

TWENTY-FIVE MILE RAMP

COLUMBINE PASS, the intersection of access roads running down to Delta and U.S. Highway 50 on the east and down to Nucla and Colorado 141 on the west, is supposed to be low point on the plateau crest and on the Divide Road — low point, that is, since getting up on top at the Massey Cow Camp saddle.

Actually a couple of hundred feet lower than Columbine is a sag in the road in the vicinity of Porter Cow Camp. By cutting in behind the Spruce Mountain ridge, the North Fork of Tabeguache Creek puts the watershed of west-flowing streams well behind the plateau fault-line front, forcing the crest farther back on the downslope of the mountain tilt. Ever since Windy Point you were driving down around this canyon head, and you didn't come up and out again on the true face of the fault until the Smokehouse Campground area.

Though lower and relatively sheltered, this unnamed sag is not considered a pass and is crossed only by the meanderings of the 47 Trail.

However, there is another named pass on the Divide Road — higher, bleaker, an over-the-hump shortcut between Club Cow Camp and eastern ranges in the days when Club spread-eagled both sides of the Hill.

Though it is not on your map it can be approximately located by the position of Club Cow Camp, by its wind-stunted trees, and by the Tongue that, stretching out below and to one side of the pass, funnels cliff-face gales directly at the spot. It was commonly used and known by cattlemen,

Pole-worm fencing at Columbine Pass. Old cowboys complained that early government-built fences didn't have enough "worm" and would soon fall down.

but until a certain, raw, near-winter day, it was never called anything — printable, that is.

J. D. Dillard explains: "Chillycoat Pass got its name one cold fall evening when stock was being moved from one side of the mountain to the other.

"A cowboy named Rich Bonneville and Charley Templeton — Charley owned a little bunch of cows in the middle of Club range, too measly for Club to pay any attention to — they had gone over to the Club beef pasture to get some horses they had over there. My Dad, who was runnin' the Club at the time, had gone out in the other direction.

"Why they set their camp at that spot, God only knows, but they came out onto the pass at about the same time, and that wind hit them in the face like a knife cuttin' hell froze over.

"Those days Alaska gold fever was in the news, and Rich, shiverin' so hard he could hardly make fire, said 'Alaska ain't the only place that's got a Chillycoat Pass.'

"He didn't pronounce Chilikoot quite right, but the way he said it is the way it stuck."

Columbine Pass, and all four of its approaches, is a flowery place in spring, summer, and fall. Lupines have it so good here they grow almost shrub size.

If it is fall when you are prowling the Columbine Pass area flower fields, you may come onto the "corrals and herds" of a very different kind of National Forest range permittee — young Rick Cooley, who pastures his livestock on the rich pollen and nectar of golden rabbit brush and other high-country blossoms. Cooley got his range rights when he purchased a few acres of private land up here on which to set his beehives.

Earlier in the year he night-trucks them to valley orchards within a fifty-mile radius of home base at the foot of the mountain to do incidental pollinating chores in the course of gathering fruit-flower honey. Unlike cows that bawl and carry on like crazy when moved from one pasture to another, bees could care less that a considerable piece of the globe has slipped under them since last flight; they sim-

Columbines, lordly in a random tangle of grass flowers, become a bushful of butterflies when a breeze sets them fluttering on their wire-thin stems.

Up the slender stem from memory banks in the tiny seed come directives that create the perfection we call "columbine." The programming is just as perfect for what we call "sneezeweed."

On the lower, sage-blooming reaches of the plateau, Rick Cooley sets up beehives
that later in the year will be moved to the top of the mountain.

ply get on with the job next morning, utilizing whatever kind of flower is at hand.

A number of beekeepers harvest plateau honey, but Cooley is the only one conducting this heavy labor as a literally one-handed operation. He turned to beekeeping for livelihood and independence after losing his right hand in an industrial accident.

"Not to say I wouldn't rather have my hand back," he quips, "but the hook is one part of me the bees can't sting."

By the time you reach Columbine Pass, if you are not prepared for camping out, you may be looking for a night's lodging. So we will take the closest route to motels and restaurants, the 25 Mesa Road down to Delta — as always, laying a patina of anecdotal history on the scenery to enrich our detour journey.

The 25 Mesa Road is the east half of an Indian Trail between the San Miguel and Gunnison rivers. Since both Indian trail and graded road occupy the easiest and shortest way of getting from up here to down there, the overlapping road has erased the trail.

At the foot of the mountain the Indian trail branched, part of it heading east to the Elk Mountains, crossing the Gunnison at a ford deep in Black Canyon by access of the Ute Trail sag in the steep granite rim. Sections of this part of the trail are still visible.

The other branch of the trail continued, just as the road does now, toward the Gunnison River ford just below Delta — yes, the same one the Spanish camped at; evidently their means of finding it. The grassy flats beside the river were a favorite intertribal gathering place. A huge cottonwood standing in the middle of the flats — now standing among North Delta suburban homes — is designated the Ute Council Tree. From the river ford the trail headed north to hunting grounds up on Grand Mesa, with social stopovers at a very fine racetrack in the soft but firm adobe clays of the mesa's lower slopes.

Columbine Ranger Station was originally Columbine Cow Camp, established by J. Frank Sanders, pioneer businessman and entrepreneur.

Like most early-day settlers, Sanders arrived in town poor and struggling and stayed that way for a while. His wife took in washing to help feed the family. Even in times when everybody was poor, this wasn't a situation to make a man swell with pride.

So J. Frank sneaked away between odd-jobs to look for gold. He found it, too, up in Ouray country — a vein so rich it made him wealthy.

The first thing J. Frank did was come home, ax in hand, and put a hole through his wife's washtub. Then he bought her some sables and diamonds. He built the Annadora Opera House over the hardware store he acquired on the corner of Third and Main, naming it for his daughter Anna and for Dora, the daughter of his business associate, Ray Simpson, the same Simpson who brought down two of the fleeing McCarty Gang after the bank robbery.

Sanders bought Delta County's second courthouse (after the third was built) sawed it in two and moved the halves onto a side street where they still stand — tall, bay-windowed dwellings, a little blank-looking on the side were siamese surgery was performed on them.

The Annadora Opera House — famous for its live performances (what other kind are there?) of Gilbert and Sullivan operas — burned down, the gold vein played out, and J. Frank Sanders seems to have just faded away.

Before he went, he sold his Columbine Cow Camp to the Forest Service. This station was the first to be linked to headquarters by phone when the first telephone wires were strung over the divide in 1908, and Forest Service fire detection was no longer entirely dependent on smoke signals.

You have been on 25 Mesa ever since you left the divide, but not until you pass the 25 Mesa Ranger Station and are out of thick timber, down off Federal Grade, do you get the 25 Mesa Road "feel," the sensation that this long skinny mesa is artificial, like a fill or ramp, made purposely to put a road on.

For one thing, in spite of its ups and downs it naturally maintains a general 4 percent grade — as does the overall tilt of the mountainside; the ups and downs naturally fall

Cedar posts, from forests lower on the mountain, are best for stringing wire fence, being slow to rot. Stock trail in the foreground connects to the three necessities — grass, water, and salt.

within what state road crews like to cope with, a gravelly 6 percent. For another, the narrow strip of 25 Mesa runs unbroken all the way down to Gunnison River level, as if it had been roughly ricked up by a super-size bulldozer from canyon material on either side.

During much of the way the road is right out on top of the slant. You can see the entire valley from end to end as you drive. And the valley can see you — in hunting season the 25 Mesa Road is a plume of dust by day and a spangled necklace of headlights by night as hunters return with or without.

What is now 25 Mesa Road was at one time the old Roberts Trail.

The Roberts brothers, Bob and George of Kentucky, didn't wait for the Indians to leave. Jumping the gun, they slipped down from holding pastures on the Cochetopa to look the plateau over and pick the best of the range before anybody else got here.

What they chose, when they had the whole thing to choose from, was what we now call 25 Mesa, along with nearby parallel mesas running down the mountainside from top to bottom. It was unrestricted range; they could appropriate as much as they figured they'd ever have horses and cattle to cover. They decided on the upper end of 25 Mesa for summer camp and range and the Roubideau at the confluence of the Buttermilk for winter headquarters.

"As the Utes were trailin' out, Roberts brothers were trailin' in," Dillard says, "making them absolutely the first cattle in any of this area."

Looking at 25 Mesa now (the lower third a barren desert) and considering that they had their pick of the mountain, the Roberts brothers don't seem to have been too smart.

But perhaps it wasn't desert then. Many old-timers have described grass belly high on a saddle horse, flowing over mesas and adobe lands that now grow only sparce, stunted, sage, shad-scale, cactus, or nothing. Carl Smith says, "Those mesas grew entirely different kinds of grass and plants than you see now." Evidently the lower lands, with their narrow margin of rainfall, could not make a comeback after the de-

vastating overgrazing that forest lands also suffered but survived.

The upper mesa may also have carried more graze then
than now. Grasses took advantage of new room and sun-
shine after the Utes burned the forests in 1879, before they
were pushed out.

Roberts Bros. brought in two hundred head of Kentucky
racehorses, and one of the first things they built was a racetrack. It lay along the flats above the Roubideau, just west of
what is now Porter Ranch. Even after three-quarters of a
century it could still be seen from the air until conservation
terracing obliterated it.

The purebred horses were branded and turned loose like
cattle to range wild and multiply. They quickly separated
into bands, one stud with as many mares and as much territory as he could hold onto. Two of these territories parallel
25 Mesa to the right, Monitor Mesa and Potter Basin. Also
named for a Roberts' stallion is Little Johnnie Spring. Not
on this side of the mountain but likewise named for horseflesh is Nancy Spring. Nancy was a libber-mare who ran her
own band over there.

The Roberts brothers brought along their own horse-
breakers and trainers, Ben Lowe and Charles Sewell. Lowe
and Sewell have been described by Carl Smith as "jingle
boys, outlaws, and troublemakers," but others remember
them as "gentlemen of the South, mannerly but temper-
some." Apparently it depended on which stage of their lives
coincided with yours. Ben Lowe Flats, over beyond Potter
Basin, is where Lowe ran his own herd and put up his
stoop-door cabin with "nothin' but a saddlehorse and ax"
during his stompin' days when Saturday night in town
wasn't complete without "shootin' up Main," which is what
"draggin Main" was called when done on horseback and
with bullets instead of on wheels and with backfiring.

Horses broke the Roberts brothers.

Dillard relates, "Roberts just played the field with his
fast horses — back East, San Francisco, everywhere.

"I guess he got to tryin' to find out how deep all the

A small arc of the Uncompahgre Plateau skyline forms the west wall for Delta and its sugar silos.

bottles were, saw the bottom of too many, and just had to back off and quit."

It wasn't until after Mathews, then Maupin, then Dillard bought the Roberts outfit that the place-name 25 Mesa came into existence. The Roberts always called it Home Mesa for their summer camp. When survey lines came through and it was discovered the home place was on Section 25, they began using that number as a horse brand. Buyers of the outfit picked up the brand, and gradually the entire mesa became known by the brand. The fact that it is almost ex-actly 25 miles from Delta to the top of the divide (often cited as the way the road got its name) is just one more of the plateau's coincidences.

Eda Musser and other old-timers maintain that 25 Mesa actually ends at Federal Grade and the remainder of the 25 Mesa Road is on Sawmill Mesa, but map makers saw other-wise. Federal Grade? A dugway financed with federal money at a time (1912) when such subsidies were so rare as to rate memoralizing by name.

Sawmill Mesa is across the canyon on your left. Origi-nally Briggs Mesa, named for another of Roberts' studs and lady friends, it became Sawmill after Sam Skinner set up one of the Uncompahgre's first sawmills there.

Sam made men of his sons quickly. When Elmer was nine and Bradford was eleven, they were driving two-team wagons loaded with lumber down the mountain to town. "All that child labor didn't seem to have stunted us any," Elmer said just before he died, old and in full possession of a headful of encyclopedic memories of old times.

Some of the Skinner lumber may exist in "The First Delta County Jail," removed from its alley location to stand in fenced honor on the courthouse lawn. This building is made of two-by-fours laid up flat like brick and spiked to-gether. In its day it contained some of the Wild West's wildest but, unlike its more comfortable successors, was never broken out of.

After 25 Mesa Road loops down into and out of the lower end of Roubideau Canyon it crosses California Mesa — named for a backwash of settlers from the Westward Ho

Delta's first jail, made of stacked Uncompahgre two-by-fours, successfully confined the county's first lawbreakers, mostly horsethieves.

tide. The place where the road finally drops off the mesa to Uncompahgre river bottom is known as Brickyard Hill. The brickyard sat on the first level ground to your left, between raw material and consumer demand, transforming great hunks of the adobe clay hill into yellow brick houses on Delta streets.

The brickyard is more famous for being the place where teenage Jack Demsey worked up the muscles that eventually made him world champ. His father labored with horse muscle, having a team for hire during the time the family lived in Delta, but Jack heaved brick with his own.

In his spare time he got in a lot of boxing practice on the local boys (since nobody had any idea what it would lead to, it was generally described as bullying at the time) — the ones he could catch, with special attention to the sons of Judge Alfred Rufus King.

King's grandson, Bill Fairfield, writes from Denver, "He used to chase my uncles home from school."

Apparently this activity was without particular ill will, and the Kings must have made a lingering impression on young Jack, because after the family moved to Denver he called whenever he was in town. Fairfield concludes with pride, "I have in my possession a sympathy card sent by Jack Dempsey after the death of my grandmother, Annie Rachel King."

Midway of the 25 Mesa Road is the Narrows where the mesa backbone is only roadwide, and ranches lie below on benches hanging above the canyons like panniers on either side.

Covered-wagon pioneer Noah White staked out his homestead here in 1903 — his is the house in the hay meadow down on your left. He and his sons dug a five-mile ditch to bring water down from the upper Cottonwood to the place; one of them died of a hernia suffered during this toil. Noah put together a sawmill and began making boards. He sawed to sell but used a lot of the product himself as his family grew to ten and the cabin grew to the present two-story house.

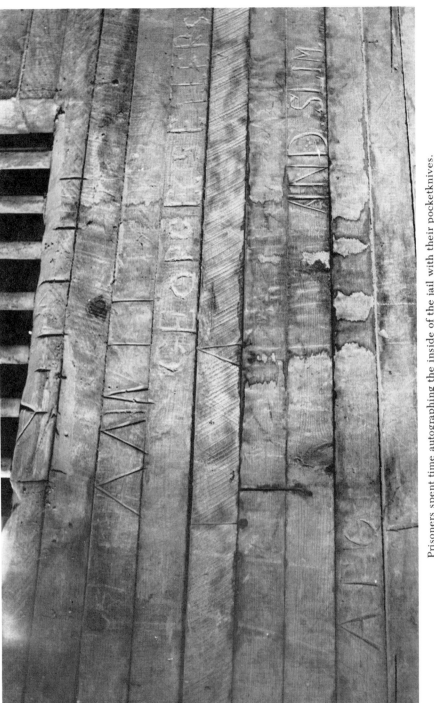

Prisoners spent time autographing the inside of the jail with their pocketknives.

He had to set his mill on other mesas because the Ute forest burn extended as far down as his cabin.

Noah's daughter, Maudie Dannels, describes the work involved in making hayfields out of those stands of burned stumps, surviving and second-growth trees.

"My brother Harry and I pulled those stumps with a mule. Guess I was about nine when we began, and Harry not much older. Father made a machine to do it — a cylinder set on end, anchored down, with a cable wrapped around it and a sweep on top. The sweep was forked to hook up both ends of the mule, and single tree behind and the bridle rein in front.

"Harry fastened the cable around the stump. My job was to keep the old mule going round and round — me and the mule stepping over the cable every turn. We'd just wind that old stump right out of the ground!"

Maudie refutes our preconceptions about the old-time inequality of the sexes in the matter of jobs, at least within the family.

"I always liked outdoor work, but one of my brothers preferred the house, so he helped mother with cooking and cleaning and I drove the hayrake team, starting when I was twelve. Then the mower, the potato digger, and even the threshing machine."

But she grabbed at domestic work when Noah offered her a dollar a day and a fast horse if she would ditch school and cook for him and his sawmill crew at a mountaintop millset.

"Part of the bargain was the horse and the whole weekend for myself. Right after washing up Saturday noon dishes, I'd ride to Delta and get there about two o'clock, then Sunday afternoon I'd ride back, arriving before supper. My granddaughter says you can't ride a horse that far that fast, but you can if you have the right horse. Or maybe horses nowadays have got softer, like people."

The hayfield and log house to the right of the Narrows are the work of Noah White's namesake son who, to distinguish him from his father was known all his life as Noan.

The tenrils of another treasure story touch the Noah White place. It goes:

In early days three men with a burro train loaded with gold (hi-jacked?) came through on their way from the mines to nobody knows where. They stayed at a cabin said to be on either Monitor or Cottonwood Creek. They got snowed in (snows here have been measured sixteen feet deep on tree trunks), and two of the men died. The third escaped only by burying and abandoning the gold. Fifty years later a man came through looking for that cabin and the gold. He told the tale, but if any White got worked up enough to join in the search, nothing came of it. If the gold was ever there, it still is.

From the piece-quilt of her memories Maudie Dannels calls up an even earlier fragment:

"There was an old woman used to come riding through here on a donkey. Once every year. It was Chipeta going to visit Ouray's grave."

Princess Chipeta, wife of Ouray, chief of the Ute nation. Tabeguache maiden, acclaimed in Washington for her beauty and breeding. Superb horsewoman who rode non-stop from the Uncompahgre to the scene of the Meeker Massacre carrying Ouray's cease-fire orders to the attacking subchiefs. Chipeta in her old age riding a donkey, without even the comfort and dignity of a saddle horse. . . .

"People used to follow her through the canyons, trying to find the secret place where Ouray was buried, but she always slipped away."

Another little girl stored up remembrances of life on the plateau, beginning with getting there via this road.

Pauline McKee Moeller describes the trip by spring wagon from the McKee winter home in Delta to summer camp near the top of the mountain.

"We would start in the dark, and it would be just getting light when we got to Roubideau Creek. Father would always drive right up the creek so the horses could get a good drink before the climb, knowing that was the last drink they'd have until the White place at the Narrows.

"I was little, and it always scared me, the creek water

rushing through the wagon spokes. Along there was the Roberts brothers place, rough scary men, and all those cellars dug back into the shadowy bank where they kept the liquor they made. You can still see some of the cave cellars. It wasn't prohibition then, but they and a lot of other people made liquor for themselves and to bootleg.

"Starting up the hill, we'd be traveling through flowers. Primroses, Indian paintbrush. There was one huge cedar tree where we always spread our picnic lunch on the grass. The horses would begin running half a mile before the tree, knowing they'd get nosebags of oats when they got there.

"Our cow camp was just this side of Columbine, a wonderful place, deep in the woods. Birds, flowers everywhere, and deer — deer wouldn't even run from you. We rode everywhere, all over the mountain. As I grew older I rode in the roundups, sometimes the only girl. My high school friends in town fought to get to come stay with us at summer camp."

There is nothing to show for Frank McKee's 1911 claim cabin. Until recently you could have seen it — the house, the cow and horse barns, the saddle and harness shed, the milkhouse, chicken house, and outhouse.

Traditionally cabins on the plateau were never locked and were never stripped bare when their owners moved off the mountain for the winter. Food, bedding, matches, and firewood were always left to tide any passerby's emergency.

As the cattle companies absorbed smaller outfits, some of these cabins became permanently vacant. For a while the Forest Service policy was to raze and burn such structures on public lands, but that isn't what happened to McKee Cow Camp.

"Some hippies moved into it a few seasons ago, probably late in the fall," Pauline surmises. "It was good weather, and maybe they didn't realize how deep the snows and cold get. They apparently tore down all the barns and outbuildings for wood to burn, trying to keep warm in the house, and then started in on the house itself, pulling out the paritions, weakening it so much it collapsed."

Leave a cow-camp cabin unoccupied for two seconds, and aspen will take over the backyard. Davis cabin on 25 Mesa Road.

Chapter XI

WESTEND ROAD FEUD

25 MESA ROAD (and its other half running down the west side of the mountain from Columbine Pass to Nucla) has a political history.

Whoever pieced out the county lines in this area must have done so from Washington, D.C., or the moon, while looking at a flat map. Against all reason, they laid out Montrose County on both sides of a mountain so high and snowy that for half the year it is crossed by nothing more commercial than deer.

More likely the county fathers from the very first had their eyes on all those taxable minerals on the other side and, by pushing the county boundary clear to the Utah line, made sure they missed none of it.

The Uncompahgre Plateau splits Montrose County into a sophisticated (for the West) urban eastend and a wild and woolly (even for the West) westend. Cattlemen and miners of the westend, rustic and rowdy but rich, felt they were being ripped off by the merchants, bankers, and politicians in their county seat on the other side of the Hill. At frequent intervals they declared their independence, threatening to secede and form a county for their own, or at least bypass Montrose by building a shortcut to Grand Junction.

Since building a road down the real shortcut through Dolores Canyon was too hairy to contemplate before the days of heavy equipment, the shortcut usually proposed was from Nucla up over the Uncompahgre Plateau, down the lovely, straight incline of 25 Mesa to Delta — Delta being favorable to the idea and expecting to profit from the trade.

From time to time (usually election time) politicians and

Evergreen needles, gold-leaf lace, and white velvet bark create the tapestry of this bit of young forest on 25 Mesa Road.

influential locals from both sides of the mountain would wangle their way up the ruts and over the rocks to Columbine Pass, make speeches, cut ribbons, and launch oily promises about oiled roads.

Application for such a road had to be made to the Forest Service, since more than forty of the fifty-two miles of the route lay inside government boundaries.

One application, made in 1916, specifies the road be twelve feet wide, have five turnouts per mile (that is, five places where you could meet another vehicle; nobody expected to pass anybody on the road) and to be no steeper than a 7 percent grade. All at a cost of $94,000. No oil pavement was considered at this time, of course. Though only a little more than four miles of the nonfederal right-of-way lay within Montrose County, the commissioners blocked it, refusing to cooperate on the ground the road would not direct traffic to the county seat.

Thus a practicable road over Columbine never happened during the time it would have benefitted anybody, though Forest Service records note that had such a road been available during World War I it would have been used to transport large quantities of carnotite, thus avoiding one handling of the ore in transferring from narrow-gauge (Placerville) to standard-gauge (Montrose) railroad cars.

The only paved road the westend ever got to its county seat swings up through San Miguel and Ouray counties, over Dallas Divide, and down though Ridgway and Colona.

Eventually enough trade leaked out the other end of the westend, when vanadium and uranium mines began paying off again on the flux of another war (and heavy-muscled road equipment was invented) to make a paved road feasible down the Dolores and up Unaweep to Grand Junction.

Perhaps it was in the expectation that sometime a "main road" would be built over the divide between Delta and Nucla that several beautiful little masonry bridges were built across dry washes in the lower section of the 25 Mesa Road. Made of cut and fitted sandstone, they were constructed by CCC boys during the Great Depression. Some of them are still there, startlingly precise and perfect in that cactus wasteland.

Beside the Divide Road, just west of the intersection with the 25 Mesa Road, is the Forest Service guard station-work camp in a photogenic swale clotted with willow clumps and threaded with pole-worm fences. On up the road is Columbine public campground, sprawling in aspens and evergreens thick enough to provide the usually small number of campers with the feeling of deep-woods solitude.

Columbine Pass is popularly supposed to be the intersection of the Divide Road with 25 Mesa Road, but the real low (9,160 feet) is a mile or so farther on.

Here the road to Nucla branches right and immediately drops down the face of the fault on the ledges of cliffs carved by Tabeguache Creek. The road is rough but can be traveled by passenger car.

About halfway down the cliff a jeep road on the right leads to the Copper King — the mine too rich to work — sitting on a bench above Starvation Point, beside the Indian trail to Round Mountain, the racetrack, and Rattlesnake Bench.

This half of the Nucla-Delta road is about as different from the east half as possible. Wriggling in miles-long detours down the cliffs and benches of Tabeguache and then Big Bucktail canyons, it switches to slightly better going down Coal Canyon, straightens for a moment in flats at Mountain View, threads Tuttle Draw, and reaches Nucla via a place whose name is simply Water, tersely indicating that things are now down to where it is very dry indeed.

A short distance beyond Columbine Pass the Divide Road rims out on some spectacular, top-of-the-bleachers views of the rest of Colorado, Lone Cone, those Utah mountains again, and almost straight down into Tabeguache Basin. Frame them over the silvery top rail of the divide-long drift fence.

The Indians who made their winter home in the vast sun pocket below you were called Tabeguache Utes. Lumped

Tabeguache Basin over the mountain-long drift fence. (Lone Cone in the distance.)

with other bands, they were later dubbed Uncompahgre
Utes, after their great cordillera-wide domain had been reduced to the plateau and the drainage of the Uncompahgre
River. Their own name for themselves, which nobody paid
any attention to, was No-ochi.

No-ochi bands had been accustomed to fighting other
Indian nations to keep their hunting and gathering "living
space," which included most of eastern Utah and Colorado
over to the buffalo plains. It required that much space to
support their existence level, or life-style, a fact they
realized acutely. They fought the white man for it until they
saw they were hopelessly outnumbered and outweaponed.

They were pushed onto prairie and mountain range
around Conejos until it was found valuable for cattle; they
were given the San Juan Mountains until gold was discovered there; they were given the Uncompahgre, mountain
and river, until farmers saw the rich, level river bottoms and
cattlemen saw the graze. Nothing much of value has so far
been discovered on the Uinta Reservation where they are
now.

Like the 25 Mesa side of the mountain, Tabeguache
Basin had its sooners. J. D. Dillard tells about some forced-
feeding perpetrated down there on a premature pair in 1880.

"There were these two fellows that had a little bunch of
stuff, mostly mining claims, a few cattle, one thing another,
in the Ouray area. They were over in Tabeguache Basin the
year before the Utes went out, looking it over to get their
pick of the land when the time came.

"Of course they knew the Utes were goin', and the Utes
knew it and knew what the men were looking for — grass
for their stock.

"Those men ran onto a little party of Utes over there
(Old Captain Billy was the chief in that particular area), and
they made those two fellows get down in the grass and start
grazin'.

"Dad introduced me to one of the two men in Montrose
a lot of years ago. He was county assessor in Montrose by
then, and Dad was kiddin' him about eatin' all the grass off
Tabeguache Basin. The man said, 'You know, Jeff, I've eat

some pretty good meals, but that grass was the best stuff I ever ate in my life. It kind of looked like it was my final meal, and I was sure eatin' as fast as they told me to!' "

The largest aspen trees in the world are found on the Uncompahgre Plateau. Some of the straightest and most beautiful are seen in the Antone Springs area, resembling tall, thick totem poles, their natural black markings like eye-of-gods keeping watch.

Trees in this campground are relatively unscarred by knife-happy picnickers. Perhaps people are beginning to realize that fungus and disease can follow the blade that initials a slow death.

Lumbering is a continuing industry full length of the plateau, but the higher southend is really timber country.

The first sawmill was set up near Government Springs on West Horsefly Creek, ten or twelve miles up the mountain from what is now Colona, down on the Uncompahgre River. Having moved the Utes successively from Conejos and Los Pinos, the government set up an Indian agency on the Uncompahgre, and the U.S. Army built a cantonment, Fort Crawford, between Colona and Log Hill to keep the Indians in line.

The army needed boards to build barracks, hospital, dance hall, guardhouse, and other civilities to meet the needs of a full regiment, so they sent a bunch of soldiers up the mountain to cut and saw lumber. The soldiers produced lumber at $40 per thousand board feet.

(Log Hill? A jut of the plateau that pinched the Uncompahgre River almost shut. Most of the year buggy and wagon traffic simply went up the creek bed, but during spring floods wheels had to go over the jutting hill. It was so steep on the downside that in order to keep the wagon from beating the team to the bottom, they applied a sort of emergency brake — a felled tree, hooked on and dragging behind. As a result, the hill became deforested and the bottom cluttered.)

The second sawmill was operated by Elisha Darling near what is now called Darling Lake on the Divide Road. Darling ran a hand-powered whipsaw mill. There were two men to a saw, one on top of the log pulling up, the other

Eye-of-god aspen trunks grow straight and tall as totem poles at Antone Spring.

The chipmunk population at Antone expects that of course you will have peanuts in your picnic basket.

Ponderosa pine is ripe, ready for timber harvest, when its pointed top has rounded
off as this giant's has.

down in the pit pulling down, in a shower of sawdust. They sliced off boards, keeping up a rhythmic beat that took considerable experience to maintain without buckling the long slender sawblade.

Private industry in the hands of Elisha Darling at once reduced the cost of lumber from the government $40 to only $14. Later operations were steam powered, the boilers fired with lumber waste — chips, slabs and edgings — and with firewood cut for the purpose. Until the modern era, the felling of trees was always by ax or crosscut handsaw. In a very few years so many sawmills were working on the mountain that competition and efficiency had brought the cost of lumber down to $8 per thousand.

As lumber companies moved onto the plateau, roads were hacked in, opening up stands of timber pre-empted under the Stone and Timber Act. Logging roads, contemporaneous with salt roads, provided some of the earliest access routes on the mountain.

Lumber companies are still making new roads up here today, as remote parcels of timber are put to bid and bought. Roads once laboriously made with ax and Fresno scraper are bulldozed rapidly and often graveled to permit faster passage of the logging trucks.

Private companies now harvest five to six million board feet per year. It is estimated the plateau has a growing stock of one and a half billion board feet.

Though ponderosa pine is the wood of choice, it composes only 23 percent of the timber. How to profitably use Engelmann spruce (60 percent) was a problem tackled early. Darling conducted experiments in making apple boxes of spruce — this at a time when fruit produced in Western Slope virgin soil was taking top prizes at world fairs. The manufacture of all kinds of shook (slats that were sold flat to be made into boxes and crates by the buyer) became a flourishing business in the days when everything was shipped in wood because cardboard cartons had not yet been invented.

On both sides of the mountain, between the upper

Stages of death. Not much can kill an aspen, but carving can. Initialing done at different times tells the story of the tree's losing battle to cure sores of spreading fungus that enters through cuts in the bark.

boundary of plentiful precipitation and the lower boundary
of practically none at all, grow the pinyons and junipers.

Pinyon — called pitch pine by the settlers — made easy
stovewood, soft and brittle to cut and break up. It produces a
very hot fire but is so sooty that women generally refused to
use it in their cookstoves because it forced them to scrape
the thick, feathery soot from all three sides of the oven every
few days.

Pine nuts, another pinyon product, were an important
part of the Indians' food supply, at least in those years when
the trees — temperamental about reproduction — decided
to bear. Pioneers liked them for snacks but usually were too
busy to spend time gathering, much less getting them out of
the cone and then out of the shell.

The pitch-bleeding scars you see on pinyons were made
by porcupines feeding on one of their favorite foods. The
pitch exudate was the pioneer's chewing gum. Try it; it
won't hurt you, and you might be one of those who like it at
first taste.

Pulverized or steeped pinyon pitch was an Indian
remedy for dozens of ailments from the common cold to
syphilis. Melted, it was used to waterproof their baskets.

Junipers — called cedars by almost everybody — are
chiefly used for fenceposts. Pioneers hauled posts out of the
foothill forests in such quantities you wonder there are any
trees left. Most farmers and ranchers cut their own, or hired
it done, but some men were post-cutters by trade. Some still
are; at almost any auction yard in towns flanking the plateau
you will see a tepee stack of shaggy cedar posts awaiting the
next sale.

Cedars resist being axed down. The wood is hard, dense,
and tough. It doesn't foul the blade with gum, as pinyon
does, but dulls it quickly.

It is just as resistant to rot in the ground. A fence of good
sound cedar will last almost as long as the man who builds
it. The same aromatic defense that repels moths works
against insects and fungus. Worms, working the cambrium
layer of the newly killed limb, leave calligraphic patterns on

Young trees begin to struggle back after clear-cutting, a type of lumbering not generally practiced on the plateau now.

the surface between bark and wood but seldom pierce the post to weaken it.

Normally juniper doesn't grow tall enough to do anything lofty with. If you happen onto a relic of pioneer telephone line you will find the tall pole is pine, grafted with steel bands onto a cedar post for endurance underground.

Indians used juniper for so many things the list is as long and improbable as an advertisement for patent medicine. Sage, acorns, and other pungent plants on the plateau were put to equally panacean uses. It would appear that, like Caucasian linaments and tonics, a substance was deemed efficacious in proportion to its bad taste and strong smell. Indian women, who delivered via natural childbirth because that was the only kind available, were just as interested as anybody else in making it easier. A month before her child was due, a mother started drinking juniper-twig tea to promote muscular relaxation.

In its early days the Forest Service wasn't satisfied with what was growing on the plateau. With dreams of making it a hardwood producer they planted test plots of black walnuts, but the trees winter-killed at 7,000 feet and below that altitude had insufficient water.

What use to make of the quick-growing aspen has nagged at the Forest Service all along. Solutions have included, boxes, excelsior, match sticks, wall paneling, and paper pulp.

Early-day clear-cutting left numerous scars on the mountain that have never reforested naturally. In some of these, and in lightning-burned areas, small trees have been hand-planted. Such projects have resulted in fine stands of young ponderosa along the Divide Road, on 25 Mesa, and the west end of the Dave Wood Road up ahead. At the present time experimental burning of underbrush is being conducted, with the aim of facilitating seedling growth.

Uncompahgre forests have a special problem — over many wide areas the layer of soil covering the Dakota sandstone is very thin, sometimes missing altogether. You will notice the natural stone-paved "parks" near or just off the road along the upper half of the crest drive. Eddie Jones,

Where nature can't make her own comeback, forests are replaced by transplanting.

who has been lumbering on the plateau for a couple of decades, explains the problem:

"Trees can't root deep where the rock is so close to the surface. They topple in heavy winds. You come onto whole swaths of down timber."

Whether the thinness of the soil is natural and long-standing or a result of the Indians' burn-off of the plateau with consequent erosion is not known — all the people who might remember what the forest floor was like previous to 1879 have long been gone.

There are no sawmills on the mountain now. The modern practice is to cut and truck the logs off the Hill in summer. Stacked or ponded at valley millsets, they are sawed all winter or all year. But in the slow days of team and wagon, hauling all the waste of bark, slabs, and edgings was unthinkably expensive. The mills were in the forest with the trees, moving as the cutting area changed. Only sawed boards and timbers were hauled down to buyer and planing mill.

In those boom construction days when mushrooming towns, mines, and railroads were lumber hungry, many of the mills ran all winter, right through deep snows.

The lumber was loaded from the mill onto bobsleds and dragged by horses or oxen down to an altitude where the snow could be coped with better by wheels than runners. There it was loaded onto wagons and hauled the rest of the way to Montrose, Olathe, and Delta and by railroad to Ouray, Nucla, Norwood, Grand Junction, and other points east, west, north, and south.

The old Transfer Road, branching off the Divide Road at Antone Springs Campground, is a relic of those lumber-wagon days. On the Transfer Road, the point where lumber was transferred from bobsled to wagon is still marked by the cement foundations of a mule barn where relay teams were sheltered, fed, and rested.

Automobiles still occasionally use the Transfer Road, but it is very rough. The tracks jog down over ledge after ledge of exposed rock strata, rather like driving down a shallow

Soil is so thin in stretches of the plateau that trees bring up pieces of the mountain as they grow.

Given time, nature provides its own nursery. This stump, cut fifty years ago, nurtures tiny seedlings (*arrow*) in its crevices.

This cement foundation of the mule barn is all that is left of the station where early-day lumbermen transferred boards from bobsled to wagon.

sandy staircase. There are better ways of getting off the mountain.

At one point the Transfer Road skirts a wide, sage-bottom canyon on whose cliff walls a number of Indian flint mines have been found.

These small caves are deeply lined with velvety soot. It is said the ancient Indians, who had no iron tools, mined the flint by heat-cold flaking — building fires in the caves and dashing cold water on the heated rock to make it slinter into sizes they could carry back to camp and chip into arrowheads, spears, knives, awls, and hide scrapers.

The mines are situated high on the face of cliffs, accessible by foot and handholds. After several people had fallen while trying to reach them, the government blasted some of them down — during the era when they were "protecting the public" by bulldozing and burning the pioneer cow camp cabins lest they collapse and hurt somebody. At least one flint mine survives.

In addition to several Indian petroglyph sites, ovens and other evidence of prehistoric life, the lower section of Dry Creek Canyon adjacent to the Transfer Road once had other attractions. It became famous, or infamous, for its bootleggers during Prohibition. Ruins of their bankside dugouts and cabins can still be seen. One was a kind of rustic speakeasy, not only producing but also dispensing cheer. The scene of well-remembered, rip-roaring parties, it is now a ranch house.

By 1925, midway in the Great Experiment, there were other mind-altering chemicals to make raids on — and at least one instance of a combination of two. A newspaper item reports:

"A booze raid in which more than the usual still, mash, and finished product were involved was staged . . . at a ranch near Olathe. Sheriff Vanaken found a thrifty field of mariguana (sic). A keg of saka (sic) was also found made from rice, prunes, and apples. It is claimed that the berries and leaves of mariguana are both employed, some being steeped and the tea added to the saka, while in another form

Indian flint mine near Transfer Road frames juniper-covered plateau foothills. Wall
and ceiling of mine are feathery with ancient soot.

Canyon wall site of Indian flint mine. Arrow marks crawl-through entrance hole. Larger, but inaccessible, window opening at right of entrance frames view of the valley shown in previous picture.

Boulder in Dry Creek Canyon, orphaned by the retreat of the parent cliff, served as a signboard for Indians.

Old cellar hole. Dakota sandstone, covering the slant of the plateau from top to bottom, provided plenty of precut building rock for Indian and settler.

it is smoked. In either form it is said to have a kick like a government mule."

Also near the Transfer Road is another "farmers folly" irrigation ditch. Dry. Never intended to flow with anything but suckers' money.

The flat end of this road approaches Olathe not far from the site of one of the West's most gruesome incidents, known as the Soapkettle Murders. A man chastized his son so severely the boy died. Terrified, he enlisted his old mother's help in getting rid of the child's body by dismembering and making soap of it with lye in the old black cast-iron yard kettle. Then, fearful his mother would not keep still about the act, he threatened her life. The old woman waited until he slept, then she killed and disposed of him in the same way. Insanity as a plea had not yet been established; the woman spent her few remaining days in prison.

Somewhere in the headwaters of Roubideau Creek, not far from Darling Lake on the Divide Road, occurred another attempt to connect Kit Carson with this area.

In 1955 a forest ranger reported finding an aspen tree in "a very inaccessible spot on the upper Roubideau carved, 'Kit Carson, Aug. 12, 1864.'

"In 1958 five men from Montrose cut down the tree and removed sections of it," the report goes on, "at the behest of the Colorado State Historical Society, Chipeta Chapter of Montrose, who planned to place the item in the Ute Museum.

"The men said they thought they were on Terry Brothers private land, but were not, and were subsequently cited for trespass by the Service."

Research showed that Kit Carson could very well have been in the area, since it was known he had had some dealings with the Utes to the northwest of the plateau at least that late.

A section of the trunk, taken just above the carving, was submitted to the Forest Products Laboratory for a tree-ring count, with the result that the tree was pronounced sound to the core but with only seventy-five annual rings. In 1864 it

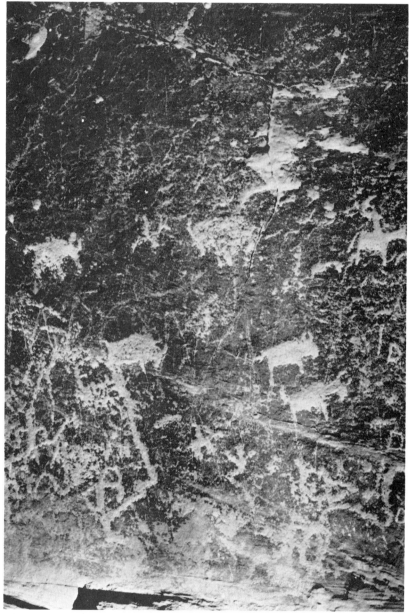

Petroglyphs on Indian signboard boulder are almost obliterated by later vandal scratchings and bullet holes.

would not have been even a gleam in the eye of two amorous aspen flower tassels.

Once more the Kit Carson-was-here myth was shot down.

Chapter XII

"DIRTY, GREASY AND WICKED"

Most of the streams flowing down the east slope of the Un-compahgre Plateau have imperceptible headwaters that are mere meadows along the Divide Road, or woodlands with a hint of slant to them. But Roubideau Creek has a source; it begins near Darling Lake — at least the north prong of the three headwater creeks does.

This prong is called Pool Creek, a name that has nothing to do with the little lake but stands for "cattle pool." Cattle pools were usually made up of several small outfits each with too few cows to pay a man to do his own riding — it takes about as much time (all you've got) to ride herd on a hundred cows as five hundred. By pooling they could hire riders, hay irrigators, and salt haulers, leaving their own time free for other pursuits such as farming, prospecting, or some other way of getting rich quicker than by one calf per cow per year.

The south prong is Roubideau proper, starting near An-tone Springs. Like other canyons on this side of the Hill, Roubideau heads downhill straight northeast. After traveling nearly halfway to the bottom in complete agreement with the lay of the land it swings northwest across the grain, al-most paralleling the crest and gathering up canyon streams as it goes — Bull, Terrible, and Traver Creeks — terminat-ing the slender mesas between them like knots binding off a fringe. It gets back into the groove again when joined by Moore Creek and is quite amenable to the northeast trend for several miles. Then it sashays crosswise once more, pick-ing up Crisswell and Potter creeks. It is aimed at cutting through the unique top-to-bottom slant of 25 Mesa, and al-

Paved with gold are aspen forests that moments ago were roofed with yellow stained glass.

most does so at the Narrows. Deflected at the last moment by Monitor Creek, Roubideau Canyon (now five hundred feet deep in brilliant red rock) jogs sharply and curves meekly away to give 25 Mesa plenty of room the rest of the way down. Roubideau has the last word, though, snatching up Cottonwood Creek before finally emptying into the Gunnison west of Delta.

Roubideau's radical vagaries merely interrupt, but do not change, the general slope of the mountain. A new set of fringing canyons — all headed the right way — is born on the downhill rims of the crosscut sections. These creeks in turn are picked up farther and deeper down, like another row of knots, by other crest-parallel streams — Buttermilk, Spring, Shavano, and Dry creeks and Happy Canyon.

Historians differ as to which Robidoux brother Roubideau Creek (it is permanently misspelled) was named for, Joseph or Antoine. Antoine has the most votes and fits the character and timing better. Then there is the matter of Antone Springs near the headwaters, whose name origin no old-timer has so far been otherwise able to explain. After all, whoever couldn't spell Robidoux probably couldn't cope with Antoine either.

At any rate a Robidoux, probably Antoine, was trapping beaver on the Uncompahgre Plateau and trading with trappers by the mid 1830s and had built a dirt-floored, dirt-roofed log trading fort on the creek a short distance up from the Gunnison. According to J. D. Dillard, who remembers seeing the rectangular log foundations of the fort, it was about where the cattail patch called the Duck Ponds is now.

This was seventy years after Rivera came through to buy furs and the soft, brains-tanned buckskin the Utes were famous for — and of course to keep an eye out for any gold that happened to be lying around. Though Robidoux must have used the popular Gunnison ford many times, he never mentioned finding Rivera's signature on a cottonwood. Perhaps Robidoux couldn't read, or perhaps the cottonwood couldn't hold up the message that long. Cottonwoods are not noted for longevity, and this one certainly wouldn't have

Roubideau Ranch is one of several on the plateau whose owners, often absent on stockmen's work, have been forced by the depredations of hunters, packers, and jeepsters, to go against the hospitality of the range and post "No Trespassing" signs.

been a mere sapling when Rivera singled it out to leave his mark on.

Fort Uncompahgre was not the only one Antoine built.

The Robidoux, father and sons, tentacled the West with a trading industry — brother Joseph's trading post founded the city of St. Jo, Missouri — mainly on the backs of dead beaver, whose fur was in vast demand for making the tall, silky felt hats then being worn by every man who could afford one. (The Mad Hatter in *Alice in Wonderland* sports a beaver, as do many male carolers on Christmas cards.)

Our Roubideau trading post was one of a string built by the Robidoux brothers. Antoine had another in the Uinta Mountains near Flaming Gorge.

Trapper society was very fluid — in more senses than one — and Antoine was in and out of the pockets (canyon pockets, that is) of such men as Jim Bridger, Kit Carson, and Baptisty Braun of Brown's Hole fame. In fact, Antoine is credited with once rescuing the men at Brown's Hole from a fate considered worse than death, arriving in the nick of time with a packtrain loaded with Taos Lightning.

Two years after it was built Robidoux's Fort Uncompahgre was graced by a most unusual guest, Joseph Williams, a Methodist preacher, who had accompanied one band of Oregon-bound church people and was to accompany another but had missed his connections and sought refuge at Robidoux's Uinta post. He described the men there as "dirty, greasy, and wicked in the extreme." Nonetheless, he accepted the protection of Antoine's company as far as Taos on his way back east.

They stopped over at Fort Uncompahgre.

We tend to think of Robidoux as a loner, skulking in a near-empty world thinly populated by shadowy nomad Indians. In reality the mountains must have been fairly crawling with men hunting things — beavers, gold, each other. Fort Uncompahgre sounds like a community center as the minister describes preaching there to "a company of French, Spaniards, Indians, half-breeds, and Americans."

However dirty and greasy Antoine Robidoux was in the wilds of trapping or trading-post revelry, when he got

Cabin on its knees in sage and grass. Forest Service policy that at one time decreed all such pioneer buildings be razed and burned now lets them stand as long as the heavy snows allow.

cleaned up to have his portrait painted he was cute (no other word quite fits), looking remarkably like Elvis Presley.

In this regard it is interesting to note that the syllables of the French name can be translated (but nobody has) as "sweet rascal" — Robi(n) = rascal, doux = sweet. The translation falls flat on its face, however, when applied to Joseph Robidoux. Old Joe, it is said, once eliminated competition by luring a rival trader into his wine cellar with a bait of champagne, rolling a barrel over the trapdoor, and leaving him there to yell and fume, while dealing the Pawnees out of all their furs unhindered.

Antoine limited his commercial activities to his fellow mountain men, refusing to deal in general merchandise — guns, whiskey, and other trinkets — with the Utes. So one day they burned his fort to the ground. He happened to be gone that day, but the men in his Uinta fort, destroyed during the same Ute uprising, were not so lucky. All were killed.

Even while Robidoux was building his fort here, the fad in men's top hats was switching from beaver to silk. By the time the fort burned, the trapper population in the Rockies had dwindled from thousands to less than fifty. The fort was never rebuilt.

When Escalante and Domiguez came exploring through here they carried the flag of Spain, legal owner of practically everything, including the plateau. If a flag flew over Robidoux' Fort Uncompahgre it would have been the Mexican flag, since Mexico had in the meantime secured her independence and possession of whatever Spain claimed. By 1853, when Captain John Gunnison's railroad survey party came through here and reported Robidoux' fort in ruins, the flag of choice was the Stars and Stripes by right of conquest and cash.

On the lower stretch of Roubideau Canyon the U.S. flag flies now over another kind of fort, the Roubideau Honor Camp Division of the Colorado State Reformatory, designed to keep men in, not out.

Honor camp work teams of men and boys build and repair pole-worm and wire fences, maintain campgrounds, and

Horizons of eight thousand years of prehistory stand in pillars left by University of Colorado archeologists working between cliff and creek in lower Roubideau.

do other upkeep and construction tasks on national forest and BLM lands. The confusing jumble of canyons along the plateau's lower fringe provides the camp with a kind of wide, dry moat, effectively discouraging would-be strayers, most of whom are used to city canyons with helpful signs at the confluences.

Also in the lower canyon is the Christmas Rock Shelter archeological dig, partially excavated by a group of scientists and students from Colorado University in the summer in 1963.

The dig turned out to be of great significance. The hundreds of artifacts sifted from undisturbed horizon levels of sand and time yielded information not previously known about the Desert Culture of the entire West, and changed ideas and dating. The great antiquity of the plateau's human occupancy was revealed in the discovery of a classic Midland Point (8,000 B.C.) in the lower levels of the site.

A climatic change had forced the people to shift from a hunting to a gathering economy. Migrating with the seasons to where roots, berries, and seeds grew and ripened, they lived out the winters here beside the stream in the shelter of the canyon wall. That they continued to live here well into the Pueblo Indian era was shown in upper levels of the excavation where pottery and corn indicate trade with the Pueblos.

The dig is named for a much later inscription on the wall. Two cattlemen signed and dated the rock: "R. P. Maupin and W. E. Goddard, Dec. 15, 1888."

Ancient basketry and the mummy of a baby were found not far from the site by local residents. These are now in the Delta County Historical Society Museum. Remnants of a Ute wickiup village are still standing on Monitor Mesa. Arrowheads from many eras of prehistoric development were once plentiful all over the plateau but now are rarely found. Most of them are in the collection of hunters.

Beyond a point near the Gunnison, the Roubideau permits travel up the canyon only by jeep, horse, or foot. Jeepsters who like thrills find plenty of adrenalin-tapping situations. In getting no farther up than Potter Basin the trail

Winter-bare cottonwood is mirrored more real than life in a backwater of Roubideau Creek.

crosses the creek fifty-five times, and some of the slants are
so steep they can be negotiated only if everybody, including
the driver, hang out the uphill side of the vehicle to keep it
from tipping over.

There once was a town named Roubideau, a station on
the D&RG Railroad five miles west of Delta.

As soon as the Indian was gone, rails were laid down the
Uncompahgre Valley so fast they almost seem to have been
sucked into place by the vacuum created when the Utes left.
Settlers likewise. Lest we think of horse-and-buggy days as
slow, consider the rapidity with which the country filled up.

Mrs. Emma Cole remembered: "The Indians left this
area September 7, 1881, and Mr. Cole and I and our seven-
year-old son Frank came here in October to make our home.
Early as we were, however, the best land was already located [filed on], and it was with some difficulty that Mr.
Cole found a ninety-acre tract about five miles down the
river, near Roubideau, that had been illegally taken up."

Roubideau station was the jumping-off place, the end of
wheels, as far as the plateau was concerned. Roberts Bros.
cattle soonered everything, arriving on hoof. Most of the
stock, however, came from Roubideau siding, pouring off
the trains and up the mesa trails to populate plateau pastures and forests on both sides of the mountain.

It is likely that during its earliest days Roubideau held a
world's record for incoming breeding stock. (Placerville
held the record for departing beef after rails arrived there
several years later.)

Naturally the chief architectural features in Roubideau
were stockyards, corrals, loading chutes, and unloading
ramps — "long as the cattle cars so the cows could get off
without jostling and knocking up their hip bones." Oliver
Nutting, who was born in the town of Roubideau, also remembers four or five houses, a general store, post office and
dance hall, providing for the needs and pleasures of surrounding farm families and a fluctuating population of cowboys.

"Punching cows was the main occupation," he explains.

When you get down to cottonwood altitudes the creeks run slower, and sandy clays settle out to form delicate tablets where the wild folk record their passing. Deer and raccoon were here only last night.

With this hint, one or more Roubideau saloons may be presumed, but memories vary on this point.

The schoolhouse was put on a hill outside the community, perhaps to quarantine it from celebrating cowboys in town after a long dry spell on the range.

When the peak of incoming livestock dwindled, Roubideau settled down to a long history of heavy shipping, as herds multiplied on the plateau and miles-long strings of cattle trailed in from Escalante and other canyons and mesas following roundup time.

Roubideau siding is still there, but that's about all.

Antone Springs and Iron Springs on the Divide Road will be your last chance for authorized campgrounds with springwater, toilet facilities, fireplaces, and tables. They are situated in two of the loveliest spots on the plateau.

Aspen trees, that are in many ways like pretty girls, seem here to be especially coquettish about selecting dark clumps of evergreen against which to flutter their finery, whether the incredible electric green of new-leaf spring or the incredibly brilliant good-by gold of fall.

Some of the straightest, most flawless aspens in creation grow on this end of the plateau — and some of the crookedest. Both are supremely photogenic, and former as snowy sculpture, the latter as antic clowns. There is no ridiculous position an aspen can't get itself into, including standing on its head with what looks like a rear end sticking up.

It has been decades since the days when deer on the mountain did not hide or run from man's approach, but if you linger quietly into late evening here — or almost anywhere on the plateau — you may see the deer slip out into open places to browse. If you wear inconspicuous colors, remain motionless and silent, and are downwind from them, they will be unable to distinguish you from a stump, though they may get curious about such an odd-looking stump and slowly walk toward you, all their sensory antenna stretched, trying to figure you out. When, after a few paces, they conclude you are inedible and probably dangerous, they will

Aspens have a coquettish genius for posing against dark evergreens to show off
their finery.

An aspen can go on living beyond the far side of almost any disaster, even a ten-ton trunk across its middle.

whirl and leap away, all in one complete, instant movement, too fast for the eye to follow, though you may be able to freeze one ballet saute for your mind's memory book.

In some public parks, more populated with tourists, deer have become rice Christians and will eat bread from the hand, but this mutually exploratory encounter between two equally free and equally curious individuals is nothing like that. It is only fair to tell you, however, that this is unlikely to occur during hunting season. Judging by their actions, deer can read bulletins and calendars as well as anybody, and they adopt an entirely different set of behavior patterns on September 30 or the day before, whenever hunting season begins. Abruptly you will find them paranoic, wily — and elsewhere. The latter goes twice for elk. Because they provide twice the meat and status, they are more hunted and more missing.

The only band of sheep (two thousand head) having grazing rights on the Uncompahgre National Forest feeds in a swath running across and down the mountain between Iron Springs and Silesca Ranger Station. They are owned by Fred Donley and winter down in Shavano Valley.

Irma Albin recalls when her husband Bert worked for Donley and when, later, they owned their own band:

"That was over in Horsefly country. Lots of bald hills and bare flats. I don't know whether sheep grazed them bald or they were always that way, but you have to open places like that for nooning and bedding sheep.

"We eventually got out of sheep and into cattle. Too confining. You have to stay with sheep twenty-four hours a day. And bears were so bad. Happened too often we'd ride up to camp and the Mexican herder would come up, shaking his head, 'Old Oso keel some more ship la snight.'"

Perhaps it was a Mexican sheepherder who named Horsefly Peak. (It was first called "Mosca" because, from a certain angle, it looks like a fly.) He did an extensive job — the name has bled all over this end of the map. There are Horsefly Creek, Horsefly Canyon, Horsefly Bench, Horsefly Ridge, Horsefly Springs, and even a settlement called Horsefly.

Leaves trace patterns of light and shadow against the texture of a fallen ponderosa.

Some plateau sheepherders have been Basques — younger sons born into the trade with thousands of years of tradition behind them but unable to follow it at home because family holdings pass intact to the firstborn. Basques are excellent herders, often natural artists (you may find a Basque pencil-drawing on a bit of board, carefully executed then thrown away) and fine cooks.

If, while preparing supper at Iron Springs, you smell something better than what you are cooking, it may be that a sheepherder has lifted the coals-filled lid of his campfire oven and you are getting a whiff of Basque braised mutton topped with Basque bread dumplings.

Chapter XIII

PIONEER COMMUNE

ANOTHER LOP-SIDED INTERSECTION occurs on the Divide Road in the Iron Spring area. Just before the campground a road cuts to the right and drops off the plateau toward Nucla, and a short distance beyond the spring is the first road off the mountain leading directly to Montrose.

The fork at the Montrose road can be a little tricky if cows or snows have taken down the signs. It is the Montrose Road that goes straight ahead: the Divide Road proper makes a square corner to the right.

From Iron Spring the road to Montrose travels fairly straight along an imperceptible divide between Little Red Canyon on the west and the headwater prongs of West Dry Fork on the east. Two of these prongs are appropriately named — Raspberry Creek for what grows in it and Bear Creek for what likes to feed there.

By the way, if you are on the plateau in wild berry time — raspberries, chokeberries, or whatever — keep an eye out for bear. Ordinarily a bear will slip away if he sees you first, but in berry time he gets possessive. After all, he knows for sure the berries grew expressly for him. If you startle him while his paws and jaws are working on juicy berries he may react aggressively. If an untimid, sociable bear offers to join you at the feast, back off and let him have it all. Should you find an adorable teddy-bear cub all by itself, remember that nature made it adorable (as nature makes all babies adorable) so its mother would love and defend it, which she will — to the death.

You may find an "orphan" fawn, but you aren't very likely to because you can walk within inches of a leaf-nested baby deer and never see it. But if you do and are tempted to "rescue" it, don't! Its mother put it there, she'll be back, and she knows a great deal better than you what to do with it when it gets gangly, adolescent, and too big for your playpen. Besides, kidnapping is illegal. Further, if you handle it, get your scent on it, the mother may not recognize it as hers when she comes back. You may, indeed, have orphaned it.

Opposite the entrance road to Silesca Ranger Station is a lovely glade pool that usually is decorated by cows lying in deep grass, chewing their cud, and waiting for you to get your camera in focus across tree reflections on still water. If you approach too near on your unnatural two-legged equipment they get uneasy, knowing that reliable humans with predictable intentions always come on four. To be ready for whatever dangerous thing you may be up to, they will rise, slowly and with great dignity. How can rising be dignifed when it is accomplished by hoisting the rear end first? Horses, you ruminate, get up front end first. Always. Was there never a rebel colt or calf that defied the genes by trying it the other way? Just once?

Cows can stand and stare at you longer than you can stand and stare at them, but their offspring have shorter attention spans. Flipping their brand-new white faces, they pretend to find ogres in the grass and go gallumping off, tails kinked and heels kicking.

A short distance beyond Silesca is the Donley Sheep Camp. This, with Sheep Creek and Dipping Vat Creek over on the other side of the mountain, is among the few reminders left on the map that bovines are not the only grazers up here.

Donley sheep graze here briefly twice during the season. Happen along at the right time and you may see the sheep moving through the liquid, sun-spangled green of the forest, darting from mouthful to mouthful, wayward as butterflies or fish, yet ever preserving the tree-hidden amorphous living shape of the flock — assisted by the authoritative voice of the sheep dogs.

Esther Stephens tells a little story that illustrates just how vital the dog's role is:

"We were down on the west side of the mountain in San Miguel country and came onto a band of sheep milling around in complete chaos."

Sheep chaos is the worst kind. Sheep exploding in all directions, imploding in suffocating clots. Panicky lambs trying to make it all go away by rushing to the tit and butting mother off her hind legs. Everyone bleating in full decibel.

"The dogs were just as crazy, yapping, dashing back and forth. A man was running around, waving his arms, and yelling. It was old Charley Hughes. He came over and leaned in the jeep window. 'Does either of you speak Spanish? My Mexican herder is home sick, and these dogs don't understand a damned word of English!'"

As the Montrose road slants down the mountain out of pine, fir, spruce, and aspen into the more open scrub oak and juniper, the views widen from tree-framed glimpses to full panoramas of the San Juan, Elks, Mendicant, and Courthouse mountains. On the northeast we see the ship-prow shape of Grand Mesa plowing into the trade winds through the ochre turbulence of adobe badlands far below.

Scrub oak, neither tree nor shrub, is wholly unloved. In a wide belt at about seven thousand feet all around the mountain, oak thickets form a barricade between lower grasslands and forest range. It is cussed by cattlemen because the upper branches tear clothing, tack, and flesh, and in general for being "a helluva place to find a cow in." It is cussed by hunters who must walk bent double for miles to follow the low runnels which game slips through so easily. Deer are nearly invisible in the grayish brown of hunting-season oak thickets, a situation tending toward end-of-day desperation shots, got off at anything that moves and contributing to an occasional reduction in the hunting population.

Indians burned off scrub oak to promote lower and more tender deer browse — and to get the deer out where they could see and shoot them. Stockmen have experimented with herbicides, only to watch the oak come back from the roots thicker than ever.

Jewel of a meadow. Its garnet red herbage has an oval setting of golden aspen and silver fence.

Twice a year scrub oak is beautiful. In the spring it puts out leaves so glistening, so intensely green, they seem to have been cut from some unearthly substance between metal foil and tissue of glass. In the fall, if all the factors of warmth and frost and moisture are just right, the leaves turn ruby blood red. Even in those autumns when the factors are not just right and the mountain oak belt is a garnet brown, there still are specimens of brilliant red — best photographed with the light coming through, not at, the leaves.

Near the bottom, the Montrose road crosses Shavano Valley, named for a Ute chief and famed for Indian inscriptions.

The road to Nucla, leaving the Divide Road just before Iron Spring, was put in by a man named Galloway, according to Forest Service records. A man whose grab exceeded his grasp — the span of his spread can be measured on the map; there is a Galloway Spring just under the rim and another Galloway Spring at the foot of the mountain.

The days of open range were also days of wide-open financing. All a man needed to become a cattleman, profiting on the use of public lands, was some cattle. All a man needed to open his own bank, profiting on the use of the public's money, was some dollars to lend. There were no other limitations or restrictions. A man could get rich quicker, and with fewer calluses, in banking — and go broke just as quick. Apparently Galloway wasn't making it quick enough on the mountain, so he went into banking in Norwood. And went broke.

The Nucla road writhes down the face of the west wall, mainly on shelves carved out of canyon shoulders, keeping its grade as easy as it can and still get down there before running out of mountainside. Snaking out of Big Red, it gets a toehold on Reade Hill, wriggles down into Tumble Creek, switches to Sheep Creek, finds enough flatland for one square corner near Ute, then goes twisting down Cottonwood Canyon to a rendezvous with history at the ghost town of Pinyon.

If just reading about it makes you dizzy, think what driv-

The Divide Road is most spectacular in autumn, a finale of fireworks before snow puts everybody to bed.

ing it would do! But it is traveled by cars all the time, with
no greater hazard than dust and bumps.

In the early 1880s the United States Placer Co., a group
of prospectors backed by British money, found placer gold
near the confluence of Cottonwood Creek and San Miguel
River, established camp there, and called it Pinyon. They
built a headgate six miles upstream, but it took eight miles
of ditch and flume along the wiggly river to bring water
down to the gold-bearing gravels they had filed on. After all
that work the yield wasn't worth the money. When the Colorado Cooperative Company came along, the Englishmen
were happy to unload the lease.

The Colorado Cooperative Company was a commune
(like the one that founded Greeley and Oneida, New York)
commonly called the Colony. It was started by a group of
men and women idealists, mostly from Denver. They
yearned to take advantage of the opportunities opening up
farther west but were too poor to do it any way but together.
No riffraff, though; you had to put up a thousand dollars to
belong. One man put up two thousand dollars, expecting to
ensure special privileges. He is the man who had a barrel of
fresh oysters hauled in over the mountain, in the days when
an oyster supper was the caviar of entertainment.

The plan was that half the members would keep on
working at their jobs in Denver, sending money to provide
materials for the other half working on the project.

Setting up their base in Pinyon and a sawmill on Tumble
Creek, they began sawing boards that eventually would
house a company office, printing shop, library, school, as-
sembly halls, rooming houses for singles (segregated), and a
community dining hall for everybody.

Each member got twenty cents an hour (payable in
shares) whether men digging ditch or women doing colony
laundry — the latter without benefit of running water. One
man did carve a cedar basin-sink for his wife's personal use
and got into trouble for such a selfish, capitalistic use of his
time and labor.

When they had no better luck placering than the English
had had, they switched from gold to farming and started

another ditch along the north side of the San Miguel, planning to irrigate eight thousand acres of good flatland in First Park.

In the middle of these common-owned farmlands it was their dream to build a town, naming it Nucla (for nucleus) because they hoped it would be the center from which the gospel of sharing-in-common would spread to the rest of the grasping world. They had their own newspaper, *The Altrurian,* where these philosophies were aired.

They worked like dogs. There were seventeen miles of ditch to build over very rocky and frequently vertical land. Having only pick, shovel, scraper, and dynamite to work with, they found it quicker and cheaper to build wooden flume along cliffs and across side canyons. The flume across Cottonwood Creek was a quarter of a mile long and sixty feet high, built in a great quarter-circle curve. Anyway, building, not digging, was their forte; a high percentage of the members were carpenters.

For flume and construction lumber to keep all those hammers busy, they set up more sawmills. One, known as the Colony Mill, later became Silesca Ranger Station. Another was installed at Ute. Like Pinyon, Ute and its cemetery is now a ghost site, but both are still on Forest Service maps.

Lumber was hauled slowly, laboriously down over rough country to the working head of the ditch project. They tried to avoid some of the team-and-wagon work by turning water into the finished part of the canal and sluicing the lumber down to the construction head. Refusing to float endwise, the boards jammed, dammed, and ruined stretches of ditch and flume before the idea was abandoned.

And they weren't through with trouble.

The Tumble Creek millset had two boilers. One was an upright without pressure gauge. According to Forest Service records: "It blew up. The engineer was killed, and his helper was blown completely out of his boots, leaving them on the ground where he had been standing, one with the sock still in it."

The people working on the project complained in *The*

Altrurian that the Denver people were stingy about sending money. They were tired, they said, of living on nothing but beans flavored with twice-used bacon rinds. They had to take time off from sawing flume lumber to raise grub money by making and selling fruit-box shook, mine timbers, and two-by-fours for houses.

The Denver people, seeing the ditch creep so slowly toward the point where they would be realizing something for their investment, complained (also in *The Altrurian*) that the workers were lazy.

Charles Diehl, the original leader on the job, became discouraged and pulled out; a man named Smith tried to carry on. Eventually M. D. Bowen secured private capital and succeeded in bringing water to First Park in 1903.

Though deflected from its purely communal ideal, the project did not fail. Those who contributed work or money, sticking it out to the end, did indeed receive shares of land and water to the amount of their contribution, but in private ownership. Nucla's communal beginning has has a continuing influence; the town is still a close-knit, neighborly community.

By the way, and as a suggestion to modern developers, they did not put their town in the middle of the rich, level farmlands; instead, they built it on a rocky hillside nearby.

After water reached First Park they all moved, and Pinyon became a ghost town. All that remains is a tiny cemetery — graves of a few who didn't live to see the dream come true.

On the Divide Road, about two miles from Iron Spring Campground, a mapped but unnamed picnic place to the right lies at the headwaters of the Little Red. Here, and in many spots along this heavily forested stretch of road, it is usually only a short stroll westward to the rim of the mountain face, with views down across billowing tree-covered benches to Lone Cone and the Utah mountains.

For the last section of its length the Divide Road still follows the watershed, but the feeling of "divide" is hard to realize — woods and tumbled terrain complicate the lay of the land. The unique clean line of the fault face blurs into interlocking drainages resembling those of more conventional mountains, but the strange evenness of the crest continues gently upward — meandering, pushed this side and that by forest-hidden streamheads, dripping and rising slightly, but continuous.

The Uncompahgre Divide Road comes to an end as it hits the Dave Wood Road broadside in a "T" intersection near Johnson Spring. The watershed does not end here. It maintains its upslope to broadside with another trans-mountain road, State Highway 62, at Dallas Divide, where the bleak ruin of an old two-story boardinghouse overgrown in aspens, some corrals, and the scar of a roadbed are all that remain of the station where the narrow-gauge railroad had facilities to wangle its little engines through twenty-foot snows.

Almost anything can greet the traveler who tops the mountain at Dallas Divide. For several summers this was the camping site of a circus couple who had staked out rope lanes for training their white terriers to fetch and carry red balls and silk scarves while walking on two legs.

Beyond Dallas, the divide (the division of waters) continues upward to the foot of Mount Sneffles, where it is grabbed like a cog cable and swooped heavenward.

Somewhere in there, invisible on the map or from the air, is the geologic fault that cuts off the plateau from all the precious metals to the south. Eerily, but not illogically, the southern border of the Utes' Uncompahgre Reservation followed the outline of the fault.

Advanced geology, aerial photographs, core drilling, sonic echoes, and all the other paraphernalia of modern prospecting had not yet been developed to establish the existence of the fault, or at least its precise location. Prospectors and miners could read the earth in their own way, and when they laid out what they wanted from the Indian, the lines fairly approximated those of the fault — give or take a little for easy accessibility. Beyond that line, the mountains crawled with men digging holes and staking out claims.

In many ways the plateau became the servant of the

mines and mining boomtowns. As we noted, vegetables and hay and other horsefeed were grown in the sunny canyon pockets along the Gunnison and Escalante and wagon freighted to San Juan boardinghouses.

Ike Traver — whose name is perpetuated in Traver Creek and Traver Mesa — raised draught animals for the mines. Horses, mules, and oxen were used to haul ore away from, and equipment and supplies to, the operation. Some actually worked inside the mines, but the preferred animal to pull ore cars in the tunnels was the burro. His small size allowed lower ceilings and less waste rock to blast and shovel out in getting at the vein. Men could walk and work crouching to burro height, but a horse could brain itself if there wasn't room enough overhead.

Some of these horses, mules, and burros never saw daylight during their working lifetimes until cruelty-to-animals laws stipulated they must spend three months of the year under the open sky. The plateau did its share in providing summer pasture "vacation spots" for these creatures.

The plateau fed the mines even more directly. It is surprising how many cattlemen got their start behind the butcher counter.

Alex Calhoun had a butcher shop in Telluride and found the miners' appetite for beef so vast he could meet it only by growing his own. As his cattle outfit mushroomed, especially after he acquired the Club, he went out of the retail end of the business. Ironically, it was mining that reduced his spread. When mining and prospecting boomed in Calamity country and he saw his winter range literally going to potholes, he sold the Club.

Dewdrop Spring is a reminder of a man who was producer, middleman, and retailer. J. D. Dillard describes the operation:

"Tom Mustin came in here on the Dewdrop, had that whole thing fenced. He bought cattle from outfits all over the mountain during the August gather.

"Cows we wanted to get rid of before they had calves, we'd sell to Mustin and not have to hold them till fall beef time. Tom would come along, buy 'em and hold 'em on the

Johnson Spring, at the end of the Divide Road, is fenced to keep cows out of the drinking-water source.

Dewdrop. He had a slaughter pen at Ouray, and he'd kill a carload of cattle a week when the mines were really runnin' good.

"They were fat cows, but we never pretended they weren't old and tough. Miners didn't seem to care. Men that worked hardrock hammers all day kind of expected a little resistance to their jaws at suppertime."

Johnson Spring, where the Divide Road ends, was developed by an early cattleman for his stock and is still so used, but you may safely drink from the pipe carrying the water outside the pole-worm fence that keeps cattle from polluting the source among rocks, grasses, flowers, or yellow aspen leaves, depending on the season.

The historic Dave Wood Road extends from Montrose over the mountain and down to Colorado Highway 62 at the San Miguel Bridge below Norwood Hill.

Dave Wood built roads and team-hauled freight just ahead of railroad tracks to a good share of the booming mine towns in the San Juans and mountains farther east. The sheer mass of freight he handled elicited his famous reply to a stage passenger who wondered if he had lived long in these mountains; "Ma'am, I hauled these mountains in here."

This quotation became the title of his biography, written (and published by Caxton) by his daughters Frances and Dorothy.

The Dave Wood Road was one of the last he built. It came into being as the result of a controversy between him and that other famed mountain road-builder, Otto Mears, in which Wood came out the better engineer.

Mears had built a toll road from the D&RG tracks near the town of Dallas (at the confluence of Dallas Creek and the Uncompahgre River) over Dallas Divide, down Leopard Creek to Placerville, and up the San Miguel to the boom-towns of Telluride and Ophir. It was a terrible road, according to Wood — who was paying Mears for the privilege of using it to freight thousands of tons of supplies into, and ore

San Juan peaks under piles of thunderheads, as seen from a corner of fence at the Montrose end of the Dave Wood Road.

West end of Dave Wood Road. Trees frame the Fuji-form of Lone Cone, whose morning shadow points toward Disappointment Valley and the Dolores (sorrow) River.

San Jaun Range spurts into peaks where the great roller wave of the plateau butts against it.

out of, those mining towns. "Especially bad across Dallas Divide and into Placerville," he said.

Taking a couple of days off to find a better route, he eyeballed a road from Montrose to Johnson Spring, down across Horsefly Mesa, to Leopard Creek, bypassing Dallas Divide altogether. It would cut two days off the Mears Road round-trip freight run and three hours each way by stage. What Wood laid out on horseback has been termed by experts as "one of the finest existing examples of good engineering from the old days," his daughters wrote, "though David Wood probably never looked through a transit."

The road from the divide to Montrose follows this route unchanged and is still the best access to the Divide Road from any direction.

With railroad track-laying crews hot on his heels, Wood had only seven years' use of the road, but it was a good seven years. He called it the Dave Wood Magnolia Route, painting this message in big letters on the white canvas stretched over the hoops of the tandem wagons pulled by Missouri's best mules.

Imagine those wagons coming now, curving out of those trees beyond the rising bend — forty-eight hooves thudding the yellow dust, harness creaking and jingling, axles chucking. . . .

If you are lucky you might not have to imagine it. Startled local residents have seen that vision become real, as movie companies recreate the Old West on the mountain. Parts of "How the West Was Won," "True Grit," and "The Wild Bunch" were filmed here.

Ruby Kaup and a friend were painting near Dallas at the close of a summer day, easels set up in the high meadow, completing sketches of the old boardinghouse, the ruin of a narrow-gauge boxcar, the weathered corrals, when a caravan of covered wagons came over the hill, as fitting and fantastic as a dream. Teamsters shouting and sawing at the reins of six-horse tandem teams as if the Indians were after them, careening the wagons along at full gallop. Not for the cameras now, just working horses, as in any other era, hurrying to corral, harness-off, and oats.

The final loops of the Dave Wood Road, west extension, wriggle down off the
mountain to the San Miguel River.

Dave Wood couldn't find enough mules to handle the booming business. Telluride mining men, complaining the ore was piling up, called on Wood to "bring in his big bulls." So oxteams were added, pulling trailer wagons and traveling in groups, each group carrying a loud bell because the road was only one-wagon wide with infrequent turnouts. A teamster had to know when another outfit was approaching in time to find a turnout — there is no way to back a ten-yoke oxteam pulling two wagons.

Wood's controversy with Mears is credited for the birth of Ridgway and the death of Dallas, both townsites on the Uncompahgre River. Dave's home and ranch were at Dallas, an important stage and freighting point on the D&RG railway. It was naturally expected that the railroad would build its branch loop from Dallas over the mountain to Placerville and Telluride. Instead, the rails followed Mears' toll road over Dallas Divide, branching from an empty spot that became the town of Ridgeway.

Perhaps another factor was that the valley at Ridgway provided more room for railroad yards, repair shop roundhouse, depot, bunkhouse, and other facilities needed by the little engines before and after they coped with the divide.

It was from Ridgway, many years later, that the famous Galloping Goose (a truck grafted onto a bus set on railroad running gear) made its infrequent run into the San Juans when mining and railroading were dying. Later this hybrid craft, or its namesake, went to California and entered show business at Knott's Berry Farm.

The west half of the Dave Wood Road slips down through forests of aspen and conifers that often seem especially arranged to frame vistas of the improbable Fuji peak of Lone Cone. It passes along great benches of grassland — Horsefly Creek and Sanborn Park — and at last, having run out of mountain, dives corkscrew-fashion into the canyon bottle of the San Miguel.

The whole route, from Montrose to the San Miguel, is now known as the Dave Wood Road, but he built it no farther than a mile or so below the crest at Johnson Spring, where he turned south, dropped down Horsefly Mesa, crossed Howard Flats, and came out on Leopard Creek through Dead Horse Canyon near Sams, an old stage station that is now called Ski Dallas.

The men and women who got off the stage at Howard Flats to stretch their legs, eat a bite, and drink a drop, were following a prehistoric tradition of the place. The Utes spent a lot of time here during the summer, trading with each other and with whites, matching horses on — you guessed it — another racetrack.

This was a meeting place long before the Utes. Flints and arrowheads found on Howard Flats predate the Utes, who stopped using arrows when they got deadlier weapons, along with the horse, from the white man.

Johnson Spring is the end of the on-top road.

You can either return the way you came — seeing new scenes — the other side of things — or take the Dave Wood Road off the mountain east to Montrose and U.S. Highway 50, or west to Norwood and Colorado Highway 141 to Unaweep and, again, U.S. 50 at Whitewater.

After the Uncompahgre's orgy of autumn color, its flurry of leaf-lookers marveling as they drive under vaults of gold that quickly become gold paving under wheel. . . .

After domestic cattle and wild game drift downward — the cattle to winter range, the game to their accustomed shelter. . . .

After everybody who isn't leaving hibernates (bears and woodchucks) or burrows (chipmunks and packrats). . . .

After road-graders go wherever graders go when they won't be doing anything for six or seven months. . . .

Then the plateau begins its winter sleep. The Divide Road drifts deep with snow and stays that way.

If you didn't drive it this year, you'll have to wait until next.